Infallible Proofs

McDougal & Associates
Servants of Christ and Stewards of the Mysteries of God

Infallible Proofs

Rediscovering the Christ Amidst the Clutter of our Twenty-First Century World

by

Harold McDougal

McDougal & Associates is dedicated to spreading the Gospel of the Lord Jesus Christ to as many people as possible in the shortest time possible.

Published by:

McDougal & Associates
18896 Greenwell Springs RD
Greenwell Springs, LA 70739
www.thepublishedword.com

ISBN 978-1-934769-44-7

Printed in the US, the UK and Australia
For Worldwide Distribution

DEDICATION

To Him, without Whom I am nothing and to all those who love Him and desire to know Him better.

Other books by Harold McDougal:

Principles of Christian Faith
Spanish: *Fundamentos de la fe Cristiana*

The MasterKeys Series:
Speaking in Tongues
Spanish: *Hablando en lenguas desconocidas*
All Things Are Possible
Spanish: *Todo le es posible*
Who We Are in Christ
Spanish: *Quienes somos en Cristo*
Secrets of a Servant
Spanish: *Los secretos de un servidor*

The Rescuing Series:
Rescuing the 21st Century Marriage
Rescuing the 21st Century Teenager

Others:
Laying Biblical Foundations

Out of print books:
I Hugged a Headhunter
Used More Abundantly

More Recent Releases:
I Can Do This

To them also He showed Himself alive after His passion (His suffering in the garden and on the cross) by [a series of] many convincing demonstrations [unquestionable evidences and INFALLIBLE PROOFS], appearing to them during forty days and talking [to them] about the things of the kingdom of God.

Acts 1:3, AMP

To whom also he shewed himself alive after his passion by many INFALLIBLE PROOFS, being seen of them forty days, and speaking of the things pertaining to the kingdom of God:

KJV

During the forty days after his crucifixion, he appeared to the apostles from time to time, and he proved to them in many ways that he was actually alive. And he talked to them about the Kingdom of God.

NLT

A Note about the Use of So Many Bible References

One of the most significant differences between this book and its predecessors is the use of a lot of Bible verses throughout. In previous versions, I used more endnotes to document what I was saying with the idea of not impeding the flow of the message with the many references. This time, my target audience is very different, and I feel compelled to document everything carefully and fully. If you're like me, you'll love the insertion of the Scriptures into the text. If the Scriptures are familiar to you, then, at times, you may want to just skip through some of the many references. Whatever your reading style, please get the message of this book. Men and women, boys and girls everywhere need to recognize these *Infallible Proofs*.

CONTENTS

Why the Key? 11

Introduction 13

PART ONE: THE NEED FOR A MIRACULOUS SIGN 21

1. Understanding the Demands of the Pharisee's 23

PART TWO: THE MANY GOD-GIVEN SIGNS 63

2. The Miraculous Fulfillment of the Inspired
   Scriptures 65

3. Jesus' Miraculous Birth 69

4. An Angelic Visitation 79

5. Miraculous Signs in the Heavens 89

6. Miraculous Confirmations in the Temple 101

7. Jesus' Miraculous Childhood 111

8. The Miraculous Pronouncement of John's Birth .. 121

9. More Miraculous Confirmations for Mary and
   for Elizabeth 127

10. The Miraculous Birth and Young Life of John
    the Baptist 133

11. Miraculous Signs in John's Ministry.................... 143

12. Jesus' Miraculous Baptism 149

13. Miraculous Signs in Jesus' Ministry 157

PART THREE: GOD'S OVERRIDING MERCY 165

14. Justice Delayed...167

15. Miraculous Signs During Jesus' Arrest and Trial.. 173

16. Miraculous Signs During Pilate's Interrogation
    of Jesus 187

17. Mysterious Darkness at Noonday........................197

18. The Unexplained Rending of the Temple Veil ...203

19. A Highly Unusual Earthquake.............................213

20. The Highly Unusual Cry of Victory.................... 219

21. The Amazing "Sign of Jonah"............................. 223

22. The Supernatural Aspects of Jesus' Burial
    Clothes.. 231

23. The Amazing Risen Saints.................................. 235

24. The Unforgettable Sign of Pentecost.................. 239

PART FOUR: What About You?................................ 249

25. What Will You Decide About Jesus?.................... 251

WHY THE KEY?

I am often asked, "Why do all of your books have a key on them?" It's a legitimate question, and the answer is this:

Many years ago, when I began doing missionary work in Asia, then Latin America and, finally, West Africa, there was a serious problem to confront. The people who were being won to the Lord, for the most part, had no Bible background and had to be taught absolutely everything. We began with subjects like "Who Is God?" and "Who Is Jesus?" and worked our way up from there. This was very demanding work and took a lot of time.

There was another problem: The harvest field was ripe, and we desperately needed more laborers, so we had to find a way to speed up this process and get these new converts into the field so that they could help reap. Somehow we had to find a way that people could mature more rapidly than normal.

I discovered that although all teachings may be good, there are some teachings that yield more immediate and dramatic fruit, and I began to concentrate on these. I was led to call these teachings MasterKeys.

Why MasterKeys? In the natural, a master key is a key that unlocks more than one door or lock. Dictionary. com defines it as: "a key that will open a number of different locks." *The British Dictionary* defines it as: "a key that opens all the locks of a set." Master keys are sometimes called pass keys or skeleton keys. They were more common in homes in former times, but they are still widely used today in commercial settings. A janitor in a high-rise building, for instance, needs a master key to do his work at night. A maid in a large hotel must clean every room. Maintenance people also need master keys.

What do master keys have to do with teachings? There are teachings that quickly open many doors to us, and I have chosen to concentrate on such teachings. They truly are master keys to greater things. This book is another in the MasterKeys series.

INTRODUCTION

A substantial percentage of the words that make up the bulk of this book were first written in an Asian setting many years ago. As a missionary to Asia, I lived for seven years in a nominally Christian nation (the Philippines), but all around me were nations dedicated to Hinduism, Buddhism, Mohammedanism and Shintoism. I loved Jesus passionately, and I wanted the people of all those other nations, now my neighbors, to know Him as I did. But how best to reach them with His message? They had a natural aversion to anything "Christian." It seemed to me that emphasizing the miraculous aspects of Jesus' life on earth, those things that proved who He really was, represented the most effective way of communicating His message to people of any other faith, and this was proven to be true again and again.

My first written words on this subject appeared in a series of tracts used in India, along with portions of the

Bible (the gospels). I spent six months in that country in 1963 and 64, and I loved it so much that I thought I wanted to go back and spend the rest of my life there. It was estimated at the time that there were two hundred and fifty thousand villages that had never once heard the message of the Christian Gospel. "That should keep me busy for the rest of my life," I reasoned. At the time, my visa permitted me only six months, but I was determined to go back more or less permanently.

As I was nearing the time to leave India on that first trip, one of the local pastors asked me to prepare a simple tract that he could distribute with each gospel portion. What he wanted was something that would help Hindus appreciate Jesus and find Him as their personal Savior. Because Hindus worship many gods, they welcome new ideas and often buy (at a very reasonable price) Christian gospels, especially during the days when they're on sacred pilgrimages. This pastor took me to such festivals, and I witnessed firsthand the desperate need. Tens of thousands of people, sometimes hundreds of thousands, were performing the most radical of pagan rites, in the hope of finding forgiveness for their sins.

Over the coming months (as I traveled and ministered in other Asian nations), I researched and wrote the four tracts—one each for Matthew, Mark, Luke and John. Those tracts were soon printed and used as planned. How long they continued in use and how many copies were eventually circulated and in how many languages I never knew, but I did receive good reports from them.

Slowly, over time, the rest of the message took form

in my heart. I was amazed to find the Pharisees and Sadducees challenging Jesus on several occasions and demanding that He produce some sign as proof that He was who He claimed to be, even as infallible proofs of that very thing were being displayed all around them. Many months after I left India, I was preaching in Hong Kong for a few weeks, and a missionary there, Ralph Bullock, who had a monthly magazine, featured one of my sermons on this subject in his next issue. I had preached the message in his local Chinese-language church, and he liked it so much that he asked my permission to reprint it. Based on Romans 11:25, the article was entitled Blindness in Part Is Happened to Israel, and it was very widely circulated. When I arrived back in the States months later, I found that my own grandfather had read the article.

By the time I returned to America after a full year of traveling in Asian countries, this message was burning in my heart, but I wondered how it might relate to the people of our own country. Eventually, it dawned on me that just as the people of Jesus' day were blinded to the reality of who He was, we had also been blinded to our own true potential in and through Him. The fact that the God of all creation chose to live in us gave us untold opportunities, and yet we often seemed blinded to those opportunities. Based on this reality, I wrote and had published a book on this subject. Originally published by Destiny Image of Shippensburg, Pennsylvania, it bore the title *Who Are We in Christ?* Later, it was re-titled *Who We Are in Christ* and re-released in several editions. The book is still in circulation today both in English (Hagerstown, Maryland,

McDougal Publishing: 1898, 1998) and in Spanish (Mc-Dougal Publishing: 2010).

Recently the Spirit of God spoke to my heart and showed me that this book now needed to be re-released in this country, this time in something akin to its original version. That startled me. What does the America of the twenty-first century have in common with Asian countries? As I pondered that question, the answer became clear to me. Not only have we experienced a huge influx of immigrants from around the world into this country in the past twenty-five years, but along with the people themselves has come their religious teachings and practices. In many cities of this great country, the fastest growing religion is now actually Islam, and no longer Christianity.

On a trip through the northern panhandle of my beloved West Virginia a few years ago, I was startled to meet up with a group of Asian Indians living in New York and New Jersey. They were traveling to West Virginia to visit the famous Hare Krishna Temple there. I had witnessed those huge Hindu religious festivals of India, and now we had the same thing taking place in the very state where I was born and raised.

As of this writing, forty-three of our fifty states are home to Hindu temples. New York and California lead the way with 88 and 57 respectively, but New Jersey has 27, Florida has 24, and Texas 21. West Virginia has only one, but it is a very famous one—the Golden Temple. It was built in the late 1970s with the help of 250 volunteers and is constructed of extremely costly materials: "Italian marble floors, walls inlaid with Iranian onyx, gold-leafed column caps, stained glass peacock shaped windows, and crystal chandeliers" (taken from www.newvrindaban.com). But West Virginia? Why did they have to locate a pagan temple in my beloved West Virginia?

Anyone who has traveled in recent years has had to notice that Asian Indians are taking over our hotel business in this country. Not all of them are Hindus, but many of them are, and they are now in virtually every town across America. Many of them have pagan shrines set up in their hotel lobbies.

And that's just a start. Mohammedanism is also growing at a rapid pace. Many Islamic "cultural centers" have been built and others are being built on the campuses of our colleges and universities. This is being done with Middle Eastern money (earned from the oil we buy from that part of the world). Astute students say that these "cultural centers" are little more than a front for recruiting our youth to Islam, and it's working. Especially our African-American youth are converting to Islam at an alarming rate.

According to Islam101.com, the number of Muslims in the United States is nearing 6 million, and there are more than 1 billion worldwide. What does this mean to us in the current war against Muslim extremism? Are our enemies perhaps camping right next door?

At this writing, Moslems have 843 mosques and/or Islamic centers in this country, 165 Islamic schools, 425 Islamic associations and 89 Islamic publications, and they are enjoying all of the benefits of American life to further their cause. Should we be alarmed?

And what about Buddhists? There are about 1.5 million Buddhists in our country, and they have working temples in fully half of our states. Again, California leads the way.

So foreign religions are growing and prospering in America, and at the same time, our people are being taken to court and sued for erecting Christmas decorations. The people of other religions are now demanding the same rights for their religion as we have enjoyed for Christianity for centuries. Should this bother us? And, if so, why?

First, we must say that we love all people, and it is our joy to be hosts to the people of other nations here in our country, as they have been to us in theirs. What bothers us is that while we love the people, we cannot stand by as their religious customs and teachings dilute our own. This nation is great because if was founded upon faith in the living God, and many other nations are poor because they were founded upon very different principles. False religions have cursed the people of many other nations, so why would we want to bring those very same false religious principles here?

We are blessed because holy prayers go up from our shores. What will happen as more and more pagan prayers go up from these same shores? We are blessed because we have loved and helped millions of people around the world and done it in the name of Jesus, our Lord. What can we expect as other religious groups utilize our American prosperity for their own causes and export their particular style of faith here and abroad?

Increasingly we are hearing people say that whatever you believe, it's all the same god. Is that true? It's not a new question. For Christians, the question has always been: Is Jesus God? Or are there many gods? This book hopes to settle that question once and for all, and in it we will let God speak and show us His *Infallible Proofs*.

Harold McDougal
Greenwell Springs, Louisiana

PART ONE

THE NEED FOR A MIRACULOUS SIGN

CHAPTER 1

UNDERSTANDING THE DEMANDS OF THE PHARISEES

One day some teachers of religious law and Pharisees came to Jesus and said, "Teacher, we want you to show us a miraculous sign to prove your authority."

Matthew 12:38

At least four times in the New Testament writings called the gospels we find the scribes and Pharisees, important religious leaders of their day, approaching Jesus with this same challenge. John recorded it this way:

"What are you doing? If God gave you authority to do this, show us a miraculous sign to prove it."

John 2:18

WERE THESE QUESTIONS JUSTIFIED?

Each of the four gospel writers mentioned this challenge at least once in his particular narrative (see also Mark 8:11 and Luke 11:16). At the time, the questions of the Pharisees seemed justified, for several reasons. Let's examine these reasons.

For one thing, learned Jews had been expecting almost daily the coming of a promised Messiah (Savior or Deliverer), since the time of their beloved prophet Moses (who lived about 1500 years before Christ), and their life revolved around the accepted fact that God would one day raise up a Deliverer, a Messiah, to save His people from their enemies. *Messiah* means "the anointed one." *Anoint* means "to sanctify or set apart for God, to make holy, or to endue with divine power." So their Messiah would be sent by God with a specific task, to bring them salvation.

The Jewish people fully expected their Messiah to be all of this and more. They believed that He would be a man appointed by God, chosen to accomplish a redemptive purpose toward God's people, ordained to bring judgment upon their enemies (who would be His enemies as well), in all His activities the agent of God Himself, and ruler over all the nations. This concept did not evolve overnight. It was built upon signs and prophecies in many generations. It eventually became so well rooted in their thinking that nothing could destroy it. It had now become the basis of thought and development for an entire nation. One day Messiah would come and redeem His people.

Now, if Jesus was this promised Messiah, how were

24

they to know? They must know, for they could not lend support to an impostor, and neither could they afford to work against the true Savior.

GAMALIEL'S WISE COUNSEL

Jesus' claims caused serious division among the Jewish people. One day a problem arose in their council when some leaders insisted that the disciples of Jesus be put to death as blasphemers and trouble-makers. Luke, the writer of the Acts of the Apostles, recorded the intervention of a wise man named Gamaliel:

> But one member, a Pharisee named Gamaliel, who was an expert in re-ligious law and respected by all the people, stood up and ordered that the men be sent outside the council chamber for a while. Then he said to his colleagues, "Men of Israel, take care what you are planning to do to these men! Some time ago there was that fellow Theudas, who pretended to be someone great. About 400 others joined him, but he was killed, and all his followers went their various ways. The whole movement came to nothing. After him, at the

Learned Jews had been expecting almost daily the coming of a promised Messiah since the time of their beloved prophet Moses!

*time of the census, there was Judas of Galilee. He got
people to follow him, but he was killed, too, and all his
followers were scattered.*

*"So my advice is, leave these men alone. Let them go. If they
are planning and doing these things merely on their own, it
will soon be overthrown. But if it is from God, you will not
be able to overthrow them. You may even find yourselves
fighting against God!"*   Acts 5:34-39

On this particular occasion, Gamaliel was able to convince the council to spare the lives of the disciples, but he
was not able to prevent them from carrying out a com-
promise plan. They had the disciples flogged and then
"ordered them never again to speak in the name of Jesus" (verse
40). Only then did they let the men go.

These religious leaders were zealous for what they
believed. They must work hard in favor of what they
felt was right and against what they thought was wrong.
Theudas had been an impostor. He had deceived four
hundred good people, and it must not be allowed to happen again. Judas of Galilee had been another impostor. He
had drawn away much people after him, and they must
not allow this to happen again.

WHAT SHOULD THEY DO?

So, what should they do about this Jesus of Nazareth?
Great crowds of their people were following Him. They
sat for hours at a time listening to His strange teachings.
It was reported that He had been forced to feed five thou-

sand men with their women and children on one occasion and four thousand men with their families on another occasion, and had done it by some miracle. The people had followed Jesus, running on foot, into the desert, where He had hoped to find a place of rest for Himself and His disciples. Before He fed them in this way, the multitude remained there all day without food, just to hear His teachings.

Much of this following developed because a respected prophet of that time, a man known as John the Baptist, had recommended Jesus to the people of Israel, calling Him, *"The Lamb of God who takes away the sin of the* world!" (John 1:29).

JESUS WAS MAKING GREAT CLAIMS FOR HIMSELF

Jesus, however, was making great claims for Himself:

He claimed, for instance, that He was the fulfillment of Old Testament prophecy:

The scroll of Isaiah the prophet was handed to him. He unrolled the scroll and found the place where this was written:

"The Spirit of the Lord is upon me,
for he has anointed me to bring Good News to the poor.
He has sent me to proclaim that captives will be released,
that the blind will see,
that the oppressed will be set free,
and that the time of the Lord's favor has come."

He rolled up the scroll, handed it back to the attendant, and sat down. All eyes in the synagogue looked at him intently. Then he began to speak to them. "The Scripture you've just heard has been fulfilled this very day!"

Luke 4:17-21

> **Jesus claimed that He was the promised Messiah, the Christ of God!**

Jesus claimed that He was the promised Messiah, the Christ of God:

The woman said, "I know the Messiah is coming—the one who is called Christ. When he comes, he will explain everything to us." Then Jesus told her, "I Am the Messiah!" John 4:25-26

Simon Peter answered, "You are the Messiah, the Son of the living God." Jesus replied, "You are blessed, Simon son of John, because my Father in heaven has revealed this to you. You did not learn this from any human being." Matthew 16:16-17

Jesus claimed to be the Son of God:

Why do you call it blasphemy when I say, 'I am the Son of God'? After all, the Father set me apart and sent me into the world. John 10:36

Jesus claimed to be their Master (Teacher, NLT) and Lord:

> *"You call me 'Teacher' and 'Lord,' and you are right, because that's what I am."* John 13:13

Jesus even claimed to be their King:

> *Pilate said to Him, Then You are a King? Jesus answered, You say it! [You speak correctly!] For I am a King. [Certainly I am a King!] This is why I was born, and for this I have come into the world, to bear witness to the Truth. Everyone who is of the Truth [who is a friend of the Truth, who belongs to the Truth] hears and listens to My voice.* John 18:37, AMP

But, Jesus said, His Kingdom was *"not of this world"*:

> *Jesus answered, "My Kingdom is not an earthly kingdom. If it were, my followers would fight to keep me from being handed over to the Jewish leaders. But my Kingdom is not of this world."* John 18:36

WHAT JESUS CALLED HIMSELF

Just look at what Jesus called Himself:

"The Bread of Life" John 6:35
"The Light of the World" John 8:12

"The Door [Gate] of the Sheep"	John 10:7 and 9
"The Good Shepherd"	John 10:11 and 14
"The Resurrection and the Life"	John 11:25
"The Way, the Truth and the Life"	John 14:6
"The True Vine [or Grapevine]"	John 15:1

Jesus declared Himself to be worthy of praise. If men and women chose not to praise Him, He said, then stones would be compelled to cry out:

He replied, "If they kept quiet, the stones along the road would burst into cheers!" Luke 19:40

Jesus said that He had existed before Abraham (who lived some 1,900 years before the man named Jesus was even born):

Jesus answered, "I tell you the truth, before Abraham was even born, I Am!" John 8:58

Jesus said that He had come from God:

"For I have come down from heaven to do the will of God who sent me, not to do my own will." John 6:38
While Jesus was teaching in the Temple, he called out, "Yes, you know me, and you know where I come from. But I'm not here on my own. The one who sent me is true, and you don't know him. But I know him because I come from him, and he sent me to you." John 7:28-29

Jesus continued, "You are from below; I am from above. You belong to this world; I do not."   John 8:23

Jesus told them, "If God were your Father, you would love me, because I have come to you from God. I am not here on my own, but he sent me."   John 8:42

Jesus said that He would return to God and sit at His right hand:

"But from now on the Son of Man will be seated in the place of power at God's right hand."   Luke 22:69

Jesus said that God was His Father:

"That's what my heavenly Father will do to you if you refuse to forgive your brothers and sisters from your heart."   Matthew 18:35

Jesus said that He and God were One:

"The Father and I are one."   John 10:30

"But if I do his work, believe in the evidence of the miraculous works I have done, even if you don't believe me. Then you will know and understand that the Father is in me, and I am in the Father."   John 10:38

Jesus said that His doctrine was the doctrine of God:

So Jesus told them, "My message is not my own; it comes from God who sent me."   John 7:16

"I don't speak on my own authority. The Father who sent me has commanded me what to say and how to say it. And I know his commands lead to eternal life; so I say whatever the Father tells me to say."   John 12:49-50

Jesus said that to believe on (or trust in) Him was to believe on (or trust in) God:

Jesus shouted to the crowds, "If you trust me, you are trusting not only me, but also God who sent me."   John 12:44

Jesus said that to see Him was to see God:

"For when you see me, you are seeing the one who sent me."   John 12:45

Jesus replied, "Have I been with you all this time, Philip, and yet you still don't know who I am? Anyone who has seen me has seen the Father! So why are you asking me to show him to you?"   John 14:9

Jesus said that to receive Him was to receive God:

"Anyone who welcomes a little child like this on my behalf welcomes me, and anyone who welcomes me welcomes not only me but also my Father who sent me." Mark 9:37

Jesus even said that to hate (or reject) Him was to hate (or reject) God:

> *Then he said to the disciples, "Anyone who accepts your message is also accepting me. And anyone who rejects you is rejecting me. And anyone who rejects me is rejecting God, who sent me."*
>
> Luke 10:16

> *"Anyone who hates me also hates my Father."* John 15:23

Jesus claimed to have angels at His command, whom He one day would send to destroy all wickedness and wicked on the earth:

> *"The Son of Man will send his angels, and they will remove from his Kingdom everything that causes sin and all who do evil. And the angels will throw them into the fiery furnace, where there will be weeping and gnashing of teeth."*
>
> Matthew 13:41-42

Jesus said that to believe on (or trust in) Him was to believe on (or trust in) God!

Jesus claimed that He could have summoned those same angels to save Him from the death of the cross:

"Don't you realize that I could ask my Father for thousands of angels to protect us, and he would send them instantly?" Matthew 26:53

Although He willingly submitted to death for our sakes, Jesus declared that He had power to lay His life down or to take it up again:

"The Father loves me because I sacrifice my life so I may take it back again. No one can take my life from me. I sacrifice it voluntarily. For I have the authority to lay it down when I want to and also to take it up again. For this is what my Father has commanded." John 10:17-18

Jesus went so far as to declare that He would rise from the dead:

"But after I have been raised from the dead, I will go ahead of you to Galilee and meet you there." Matthew 26:32

"All right," Jesus replied. "Destroy this temple, and in three days I will raise it up."
"What!" they exclaimed. "It has taken forty-six years to build this Temple, and you can rebuild it in three days?" But when Jesus said "this temple," he meant his own body. John 2:19-21

Jesus declared that His words would never pass away, even though Heaven and Earth *would* eventually pass:

*"Heaven and earth will disappear, but my words will
never disappear."*   Mark 13:31

(see also Luke 21:33)

Jesus commanded His disciples to teach to the people
of all other nations all the things He had taught them,
to baptize any new disciples in His name (as well as
that of the Father) and that He would always be with
them as they carried out this all-important work:

*"Therefore, go and make disciples of all the nations,
baptizing them in the name of the Father and the Son
and the Holy Spirit. Teach these new disciples to obey
all the commands I have given you. And be sure of this:
I am with you always, even to the end of the age."*

Matthew 28:19-20

Jesus' words were, He said, *"spirit and life"*:

*"And the very words I have spoken to you are spirit and
life."*   John 6:63

Jesus' words, He claimed, would be the basis of judgment on the final day of God's reckoning with mankind:

*"But all who reject me and my message will be judged on
the day of judgment by the truth I have spoken."*

John 12:48

Jesus said that God had given Him all power (authority),
both in Heaven and on Earth:

> *Jesus' words, He claimed, would be the basis of judgment on the final day of God's reckoning with mankind!*

Jesus came and told his disciples, "I have been given all authority in heaven and on earth."
Matthew 28:18

Jesus said that no one could know God unless they received Him (Jesus) first:

"My Father has entrusted everything to me. No one truly knows the Son except the Father, and no one truly knows the Father except the Son and those to whom the Son chooses to reveal him."
Matthew 11:27

Jesus said that *"the keys of the Kingdom of Heaven"* were at His disposal to give to whomever He wished:

"And I will give you the keys of the Kingdom of Heaven. Whatever you forbid on earth will be forbidden in heaven, and whatever you permit on earth will be permitted in heaven."
Matthew 16:19

Jesus said that He had come to Earth to offer men *"a rich and satisfying life"*:

> *"The thief's purpose is to steal and kill and destroy. My purpose is to give them a rich and satisfying life."*
> John 10:10

Jesus said that He had living water, and if a person drank of this water he or she would never thirst again:

> *Jesus replied, "Anyone who drinks this [well] water will soon become thirsty again. But those who drink the water I give will never be thirsty again. It becomes a fresh, bubbling spring within them, giving them eternal life."*
> John 4:13-14

Jesus claimed to be able to give rest to the weary:

> *Then Jesus said, "Come to me, all of you who are weary and carry heavy burdens, and I will give you rest. Take my yoke upon you. Let me teach you, because I am humble and gentle at heart, and you will find rest for your souls."*
> Matthew 11:28-29

Jesus claimed that to believe on Him was to do the work of God:

> *Jesus told them, "This is the only work God wants from you: Believe in the one he has sent."* John 6:29

37

Jesus likened those who obeyed His teachings to a wise
man who built his house on a solid foundation:

> *"Anyone who listens to my teaching and follows it is wise,*
> *like a person who builds a house on solid rock. Though the*
> *rain comes in torrents and the floodwaters rise and the winds*
> *beat against that house, it won't collapse because it is built*
> *on bedrock."*   Matthew 7:24-25

> *"I will show you what it's like when someone comes to*
> *me, listens to my teaching, and then follows it. It is like*
> *a person building a house who digs deep and lays the*
> *foundation on solid rock. When the floodwaters rise and*
> *break against that house, it stands firm because it is well*
> *built."*   Luke 6:47-48

Jesus taught that those who loved and obeyed Him
would be loved and blessed (or honored) by God:

> *"And the Father will honor anyone who serves me."*
>   John 12:26

> *"Those who accept my commandments and obey them*
> *are the ones who love me. And because they love me, my*
> *Father will love them. And I will love them and reveal*
> *myself to each of them."*   John 14:21

Jesus taught that He would consider to be His brother,
His sister and His mother all those who did the will of
His heavenly Father:

"Anyone who does the will of my Father in heaven is my brother and sister and mother!"   Matthew 12:50

Jesus even taught that a person who would lose his or her life for His sake would find real life:

"If you cling to your life, you will lose it; but if you give up your life for me, you will find it."   Matthew 10:39

"If you try to hang on to your life, you will lose it. But if you give up your life for my sake, you will save it."
Matthew 16:25

Jesus promised His twelve closest followers twelve thrones in Heaven:

Jesus replied, "I assure you that when the world is made new and the Son of Man sits upon his glorious throne, you who have been my followers will also sit on twelve thrones, judging the twelve tribes of Israel."
Matthew 19:28

Jesus promised that those who would forsake houses, lands, and families for Him would receive a hundred times as much in return, as well as the promise of ever-lasting life to come:

"And everyone who has given up houses or brothers or sisters or father or mother or children or property, for my

sake, will receive a hundred times as much in return and will inherit eternal life. Matthew 19:29

"I assure you that everyone who has given up house or brothers or sisters or mother or father or children or property, for my sake and for the Good News, will receive now in return a hundred times as many houses, brothers, sisters, mothers, children, and property—along with persecution. And in the world to come that person will have eternal life." Mark 10:29-30

Jesus said that He would raise from the dead *"at the last day"* those who have believed on Him:

"And this is the will of God, that I should not lose even one of all those he has given me, but that I should raise them up at the last day. For it is my Father's will that all who see his Son and believe in him should have eternal life. I will raise them up at the last day." John 6:39-40

"For no one can come to me unless the Father who sent me draws them to me, and at the last day I will raise them up." John 6:44

Jesus even stated, mysteriously, that if a person would keep His sayings, they would *"never die"*:

"I tell you the truth, anyone who obeys my teaching will never die!" John 8:51

"My sheep listen to my voice; I know them, and they follow me. I give them eternal life, and they will never perish. No one can snatch them away from me." John 10:27-28

Jesus told His followers to use His name in prayer and promised that doing so would bring results:

> *"You can ask for anything in my name, and I will do it, so that the Son can bring glory to the Father. Yes, ask me for anything in my name, and I will do it!"*
> John 14:13-14

> *"You didn't choose me. I chose you. I appointed you to go and produce lasting fruit, so that the Father will give you whatever you ask for, using my name."* John 15:16

> *"At that time you won't need to ask me for anything. I tell you the truth, you will ask the Father directly, and he will grant your request because you use my name."* John 16:23

> *Jesus told His followers to use His name in prayer and promised that doing so would bring results!*

Jesus told His followers to ask for whatever they needed and wanted, and it would be given to them by God:

"But if you remain in me and my words remain in you, you may ask for anything you want, and it will be granted!" John 15:7

Jesus warned that anyone who would offend His followers would be in danger of judgment:

And whosoever shall offend one of these little ones that believe in me, it is better for him that a millstone were hanged about his neck, and he were cast into the sea.
Mark 9:42, KJV

Jesus likened those who rejected His teachings to a foolish man who built his house on a poor foundation, unable to stand the test of life's storms:

"But anyone who hears my teaching and doesn't obey it is foolish, like a person who builds a house on sand. When the rains and floods come and the winds beat against that house, it will collapse with a mighty crash."
Matthew 7:26-27

"But anyone who hears and doesn't obey is like a person who builds a house without a foundation. When the floods sweep down against that house, it will collapse into a heap of ruins."
Luke 6:49

Jesus warned that whoever would be ashamed to openly confess Him before others would find Him (Jesus) ashamed to confess that person's name before His Father and the angels of Heaven:

"If anyone is ashamed of me and my message in these adulterous and sinful days, the Son of Man will be ashamed of that person when he returns in the glory of his Father with the holy angels."   Mark 8:38
(see also Luke 9:26)

"I tell you the truth, everyone who acknowledges me publicly here on earth, the Son of Man will also acknowledge in the presence of God's angels. But anyone who denies me here on earth will be denied before God's angels."
Luke 12:8-9

Jesus stated that whoever did not believe in Him would *"die in [their] sins"*:

"Unless you believe that I Am who I claim to be, you will die in your sins."   John 8:24

Separated from Him, Jesus asserted, no one could live a fruitful life:

"Remain in me, and I will remain in you. For a branch cannot produce fruit if it is severed from the vine, and you cannot be fruitful unless you remain in me." John 15:4

Jesus went even further by stating:

"Apart from me you can do nothing."   John 15:5

> *If the claims of Jesus were not true, then He was the greatest liar and deceiver ever to walk the face of the earth!*

Jesus said, on several occasions, that burning fire awaited those who did not abide (or remain) in Him:

"Anyone who does not remain in me is thrown away like a useless branch and withers. Such branches are gathered into a pile to be burned."
                                        John 15:6

Wow! Such powerful claims! But was it all true or not? If the claims of Jesus were not true, then He was the greatest liar and deceiver ever to walk the face of the earth. This was the dilemma that faced the Pharisees and other religious leaders of His day. Was He the promised Messiah? Or was He a blasphemer? A sign would give them the answer, one way or the other. They needed a sign from Heaven. Therefore they insisted, *"We want you to show us a miraculous sign to prove your authority."* In a very real sense, they appeared to be justified in these demands.

44

THEY HAD BEEN TOLD TO ASK FOR A SIGN

Another reason the religious leaders of Jesus' day felt justified in questioning Him in this way can be found in the words of the prophet Isaiah, spoken to Ahaz, King of Judah, seven hundred years earlier. He said:

> *"Ask the Lord your God for a sign of confirmation, Ahaz. Make it as difficult as you want — as high as heaven or as deep as the place of the dead."* Isaiah 7:11

Other translations do not include the personal name, so that this command was later considered to be for all of Israel:

> *"Ask a sign for yourself from the LORD your God; ask it either in the depth or in the height above."* NKJ

The anointed words of Isaiah had been recorded for future generations and were recognized as part of the sacred Scriptures, not just for the people of his day, but for all people of all times. This gave the religious leaders of Jesus' day reason to question Him. God Himself had commanded them to do it.

GOD OFTEN SPOKE THROUGH MIRACULOUS SIGNS

A third reason the Pharisees were justified in their challenge to Jesus is that it was customary, in God's dealings with His people, to speak to them through miraculous signs. For instance, in Genesis, we read of a miraculous sign that God gave to the prophet Noah:

> Then God said, "I am giving you a sign of my covenant with you and with all living creatures, for all generations to come. I have placed my rainbow in the clouds. It is the sign of my covenant with you and with all the earth."
>
> Genesis 9:12-13

Exodus tells of two supernatural signs and the promise of more to come that God gave to Moses before he had to appear before Pharaoh, King of Egypt, and a series of great signs that God gave to Pharaoh himself by the hand of Moses.

The signs to Moses:

> Then the Lord asked him, "What is that in your hand?"
> "A shepherd's staff," Moses replied.
> "Throw it down on the ground," the Lord told him. So Moses threw down the staff, and it turned into a snake! Moses jumped back.
> Then the Lord told him, "Reach out and grab its tail." So Moses reached out and grabbed it, and it turned back into a shepherd's staff in his hand.
> "Perform this sign," the Lord told him. "Then they will believe that the Lord, the God of their ancestors—the God of Abraham, the God of Isaac, and the God of Jacob—really has appeared to you."
> Then the Lord said to Moses, "Now put your hand inside your cloak." So Moses put his hand inside his cloak, and

when he took it out again, his hand was white as snow with a severe skin disease. "Now put your hand back into your cloak," the Lord said. So Moses put his hand back in, and when he took it out again, it was as healthy as the rest of his body.

The Lord said to Moses, "If they do not believe you and are not convinced by the first miraculous sign, they will be convinced by the second sign. And if they don't believe you or listen to you even after these two signs, then take some water from the Nile River and pour it out on the dry ground. When you do, the water from the Nile will turn to blood on the ground." Exodus 4:2-9

The signs to Pharaoh:

"But I will make Pharaoh's heart stubborn so I can multiply my miraculous signs and wonders in the land of Egypt."

"Pharaoh will demand, 'Show me a miracle.' When he does this, say to Aaron, 'Take your staff and throw it down in front of Pharaoh, and it will become a serpent.' "

Exodus 7:3 and 9

So this is what the Lord says: "I will show you that I am the Lord." Look! I will strike the water of the Nile with this staff in my hand, and the river will turn to blood.

Exodus 7:17

"If you refuse to let them go, I will send a plague of frogs across your entire land." Exodus 8:2

47

"You set the time!" Moses replied. "Tell me when you want me to pray for you, your officials, and your people. Then you and your houses will be rid of the frogs. They will remain only in the Nile River."

"Do it tomorrow," Pharaoh said.

"All right," Moses replied, "it will be as you have said. Then you will know that there is no one like the Lord our God. The frogs will leave you and your houses, your officials, and your people. They will remain only in the Nile River."   Exodus 8:9-11

So the Lord said to Moses, "Tell Aaron, 'Raise your staff and strike the ground. The dust will turn into swarms of gnats throughout the land of Egypt.' "   Exodus 8:16

"If you [Pharaoh] refuse, then I will send swarms of flies on you, your officials, your people, and all the houses. The Egyptian homes will be filled with flies, and the ground will be covered with them. But this time I will spare the region of Goshen, where my people live. No flies will be found there. Then you will know that I am the Lord and that I am present even in the heart of your land. I will make a clear distinction between my people and your people. This miraculous sign will happen tomorrow."   Exodus 8:21-23

"The hand of the Lord will strike all your livestock—your horses, donkeys, camels, cattle, sheep, and goats—with a deadly plague. But the Lord will again make a distinc-

tion between the livestock of the Israelites and that of the Egyptians. Not a single one of Israel's animals will die!

Exodus 9:3-4

"The ashes will spread like fine dust over the whole land of Egypt, causing festering boils to break out on people and animals throughout the land."

So they took soot from a brick kiln and went and stood before Pharaoh. As Pharaoh watched, Moses threw the soot into the air, and boils broke out on people and animals alike. Even the magicians were unable to stand before Moses, because the boils had broken out on them and all the Egyptians.   Exodus 9:9-11

"If you don't, I will send more plagues on you and your officials and your people. Then you will know that there is no one like me in all the earth. By now I could have lifted my hand and struck you and your people with a plague to wipe you off the face of the earth.

Exodus 9:14-15

> "Then you will know that there is no one like the Lord our God!"

"So tomorrow at this time I will send a hailstorm more devastating than any in all the history of Egypt. Quick! Order your livestock and servants to come in from the

49

fields to find shelter. Any person or animal left outside will die when the hail falls."   Exodus 9:18-19

"If you refuse, watch out! For tomorrow I will bring a swarm of locusts on your country."   Exodus 10:4

Then the Lord said to Moses, "Lift your hand toward heaven, and the land of Egypt will be covered with a darkness so thick you can feel it."   Exodus 10:21

"All the firstborn sons will die in every family in Egypt, from the oldest son of Pharaoh, who sits on his throne, to the oldest son of his lowliest servant girl who grinds the flour. Even the firstborn of all the livestock will die. Then a loud wail will rise throughout the land of Egypt, a wail like no one has heard before or will ever hear again. But among the Israelites it will be so peaceful that not even a dog will bark. Then you will know that the Lord makes a distinction between the Egyptians and the Israelites."   Exodus 11:5-7

Judges tells of several great signs God gave to the warrior Gideon:

Gideon replied, "If you are truly going to help me, show me a sign to prove that it is really the Lord speaking to me. Don't go away until I come back and bring my offering to you."
He answered, "I will stay here until you return."

Gideon hurried home. He cooked a young goat, and with a basket of flour he baked some bread without yeast. Then, carrying the meat in a basket and the broth in a pot, he brought them out and presented them to the angel, who was under the great tree.

The angel of God said to him, "Place the meat and the unleavened bread on this rock, and pour the broth over it." And Gideon did as he was told. Then the angel of the Lord touched the meat and bread with the tip of the staff in his hand, and fire flamed up from the rock and consumed all he had brought. And the angel of the Lord disappeared.　　　　　　　　　Judges 6:17-21

Then Gideon said to God, "If you are truly going to use me to rescue Israel as you promised, prove it to me in this way. I will put a wool fleece on the threshing floor tonight. If the fleece is wet with dew in the morning but the ground is dry, then I will know that you are going to help me rescue Israel as you promised." And that is just what happened. When Gideon got up early the next morning, he squeezed the fleece and wrung out a whole bowlful of water.

Then Gideon said to God, "Please don't be angry with me, but let me make one more request. Let me use the fleece for one more test. This time let the fleece remain dry while the ground around it is wet with dew." So that night God did as Gideon asked. The fleece was dry in the morning, but the ground was covered with dew.　　　　　　　　　Judges 6:36-40

51

The book of First Samuel records miraculous signs to Eli, the then current judge over Israel, to Saul, the first king over Israel, and to Jonathan his son.

The sign to Eli:

"This time let the fleece remain dry while the ground around it is wet with dew!"

"And to prove that what I have said will come true, I will cause your two sons, Hophni and Phinehas, to die on the same day!" 1 Samuel 2:34

The sign to Saul:

"After these signs take place, do what must be done, for God is with you. Then go down to Gilgal ahead of me. I will join you there to sacrifice burnt offerings and peace offerings. You must wait for seven days until I arrive and give you further instructions."
As Saul turned and started to leave, God gave him a new heart, and all Samuel's signs were fulfilled that day. 1 Samuel 10:7-9

The sign to Jonathan:

"But if they say, 'Come on up and fight,' then we will go up. That will be the Lord's sign that he will help us defeat them." 1 Samuel 14:10

First Kings records a sign God gave to King Jeroboam:

That same day the man of God gave a sign to prove his message. He said, "The Lord has promised to give this sign: This altar will split apart, and its ashes will be poured out on the ground."

When King Jeroboam heard the man of God speaking against the altar at Bethel, he pointed at him and shouted, "Seize that man!" But instantly the king's hand became paralyzed in that position, and he couldn't pull it back. At the same time a wide crack appeared in the altar, and the ashes poured out, just as the man of God had predicted in his message from the Lord. 1 Kings 13:3-5

Second Kings, Second Chronicles and Isaiah all narrate two signs given to King Hezekiah. The first sign to Hezekiah:

Then Isaiah said to Hezekiah, "Here is the proof that what I say is true:

"This year you will eat only what grows up by itself, and next year you will eat what springs up from that.

But in the third year you will plant crops and harvest them; you will tend vineyards and eat their fruit. 2 Kings 19:29
(see also Isaiah 37:30)

The second sign to Hezekiah:

Meanwhile, Hezekiah had said to Isaiah, "What sign will the Lord give to prove that he will heal me and that I will go to the Temple of the Lord three days from now?"

53

Isaiah replied, "This is the sign from the Lord to prove that he will do as he promised. Would you like the shadow on the sundial to go forward ten steps or backward ten steps?"

"The shadow always moves forward," Hezekiah replied, "so that would be easy. Make it go ten steps backward instead." So Isaiah the prophet asked the Lord to do this, and he caused the shadow to move ten steps backward on the sundial of Ahaz!   2 Kings 20:8-11

(see also Isaiah 38:7-8)

About that time Hezekiah became deathly ill. He prayed to the Lord, who healed him and gave him a miraculous sign. But Hezekiah did not respond appropriately to the kindness shown him, and he became proud. So the Lord's anger came against him and against Judah and Jerusalem. Then Hezekiah humbled himself and repented of his pride, as did the people of Jerusalem. So the Lord's anger did not fall on them during Hezekiah's lifetime.

2 Chronicles 32:24-26

(see also Isaiah 38:22)

Isaiah became a sign himself, to the people of Israel on one occasion and to Egypt and Ethiopia on another:

"I and the children the Lord has given me serve as signs and warnings to Israel from the Lord of Heaven's Armies who dwells in his Temple on Mount Zion."

Isaiah 8:18

Then the Lord said, "My servant Isaiah has been walking around naked and barefoot for the last three years. This is a sign—a symbol of the terrible troubles I will bring upon Egypt and Ethiopia."   Isaiah 20:3

Ezekiel also was used to bring signs to the nation of Israel:

"Then take an iron griddle and place it between you and the city. Turn toward the city and demonstrate how harsh the siege will be against Jerusalem. This will be a warning [a sign] to the people of Israel."   Ezekiel 4:3

"As they watch, lift your pack to your shoulders and walk away into the night. Cover your face so you cannot see the land you are leaving. For I have made you a sign for the people of Israel."
So I did as I was told. In broad daylight I brought my pack outside, filled with the things I might carry into exile. Then in the evening while the people looked on, I dug through the wall with my hands and went out into the night with my pack on my shoulder.
The next morning this message came to me from the Lord: "Son of man, these rebels, the people of Israel, have asked you what all this means. Say to them, 'This is what the Sovereign Lord says: These actions contain a message for King Zedekiah in Jerusalem and for all the people of Israel.' Explain that your actions are a sign to show what will soon happen to them, for they will be driven into exile as captives."   Ezekiel 12:6-11

"Ezekiel is an example [sign] for you; you will do just as he has done. And when that time comes, you will know that I am the Lord."   Ezekiel 24:24

"And when he arrives, your voice will suddenly return so you can talk to him, and you will be a symbol [sign] for these people. Then they will know that I am the Lord."   Ezekiel 24:27

King Nebuchadnezzar of the Babylonian Empire spoke of signs that God, in His mercy, had shown him:

"I want you all to know about the miraculous signs and wonders the Most High God has performed for me.
How great are his signs,
how powerful his wonders!
His kingdom will last forever,
his rule through all generations."   Daniel 4:2-3

The prophet Daniel received signs:

He rescues and saves his people;
he performs miraculous signs and wonders
in the heavens and on earth.
He has rescued Daniel
from the power of the lions."   Daniel 6:27

STILL MORE SIGNS

The Bible also records the following signs:

The Passover sign	Exodus 13:9
The Sabbath sign	Exodus 31:13, Ezekiel 20:12 and 20
Signs in the wilderness	Numbers 14:11 and Joshua 24:17
The censers sign	Numbers 16:38
The sign of judgment	Numbers 26:10
False signs	Deuteronomy 13:1-3
Curses as signs	Deuteronomy 28:45-48
A sign of fire	Jeremiah 6:1
Captivity as a sign	Jeremiah 44:29-30

One of the original purposes of the sun, moon and stars was for signs to God's people:

Then God said, "Let there be lights in the firmament of the heavens to divide the day from the night; and let them be for signs and seasons, and for days and years."
Genesis 1:14, NKJ

Thus says the Lord:

"Do not learn the way of the Gentiles;
Do not be dismayed at the signs of heaven,
For the Gentiles are dismayed at them." Jeremiah 10:2, NKJ

And when that time comes, you will know that I am the Lord!

Finally, when God ceased to give signs, those who understood their importance and noticed their absence began to worry about it. They knew that something must be wrong or God would be speaking to them as He always had:

"We do not see our signs;
There is no longer any prophet;
Nor is there any among us who knows how long."

Psalm 74:9

SO, WAS THE QUESTIONING OF JESUS NOT NATURAL?

Given all of this, was it not natural that the religious leaders of Jesus' day expected God to give them some miraculous sign concerning this most important event in their history, the coming of Messiah? They must have some means of knowing the real Savior from the impostors. Since the prophet Isaiah challenged God's people to seek signs and God frequently spoke to them through signs, we must conclude that they were justified in approaching Jesus with their challenge: *"We want you to show us a miraculous sign to prove your authority."*

But if the first-century leaders were justified in challenging the claims of Jesus, why, then, was He angry with them? Why did He call them *"an evil, adulterous generation"* and why did He refuse to show them any sign, except a vague promise of some future sign, which He called *"the sign of the prophet Jonah"*?

But Jesus replied, "Only an evil, adulterous generation would demand a miraculous sign; but the only sign I will give them is the sign of the prophet Jonah."

Matthew 12:39

What was really going on here? Was Jesus afraid? Was He unable to meet the challenges of these Jewish leaders? Was He, after all, just an ordinary man, an impostor, a fake?

If the scribes and Pharisees were justified, why did the gospel writers Mark and Luke both depict them as insincere and only *"testing [or tempting]"* Jesus?

When the Pharisees heard that Jesus had arrived, they came and started to argue with him. Testing him, they demanded that he show them a miraculous sign from heaven to prove his authority. Mark 8:11

Others, trying to test Jesus, demanded that he show them a miraculous sign from heaven to prove his authority.

Luke 11:16

These are the words of sacred Scripture. Does this mean that the Bible is fake too? Is it just the imagination of the minds of vain individuals? Were its writers only conspirators in a plot hatched by Jesus or His promoters?

The answers to these questions are of life and death importance, for as we have seen, Jesus taught that if men and women rejected Him they would be lost eternally. If He was right, much of the populous of our world will perish. He taught that everyone must one day stand before God and

59

> *If the scribes and Pharisees were justified, why did the gospel writers Mark and Luke both depict them as insincere and only "testing [or tempting]" Jesus?*

give account of his or her deeds. Only those who have accepted Him as Savior, He claimed, would escape the wrath of God. And, as we have seen, He went even further by stating that His Word would be the only basis for all judgment on that day of reckoning.

What, then, can we say about this all-important truth? The fact is that history, science and experience all support both Jesus and His Word, the Holy Bible. He was not afraid of the challenges of the religious leaders of His day. He was more than capable of meeting their every challenge, for He was the Son of God, the Savior of the world. Jesus of Nazareth was not just another good man, another prophet of God or teacher of righteousness. He was God Himself, veiled in human flesh, lowering Himself to the abode of sinners, that He might save those who were willing to receive Him.

WHY WAS JESUS ANGRY?

Then why was Jesus angry with those who challenged His power?

The answer is that He was not angry because they challenged His power. He was always ready to reveal His power openly, so that people might believe on Him and be saved. And He was certainly not angry with them for following the admonition of the prophets. He fully supported the Scriptures, just as they supported Him.

Why, then? Jesus was angry with the first-century scribes and Pharisees because they were hypocrites. Their sincerity was a pretense. They were not seeking truth from Him, Whom they sarcastically called *"Master (Teacher)."* They were only tempting Him, trying to get Him to say something that could be used against Him before the council. They fully intended to have Him put to death. They wanted His silenced.

Jesus was angry with the first-century religious leaders, not because they sought a sign, but because He had already given them a multitude of signs, and they had rejected all of them. Now, let's go back and look at some of those miraculous signs, those *Infallible Proofs* so that we can judge for ourselves.

PART TWO

THE MANY SIGNS GIVEN

CHAPTER 2

THE MIRACULOUS FULFILLMENT OF THE INSPIRED SCRIPTURES

Above all, you must realize that no prophecy in Scripture ever came from the prophet's own understanding, or from human initiative. No, those prophets were moved by the Holy Spirit, and they spoke from God. 2 Peter 1:21

One of the greatest of the miraculous signs given by God to His people were the Scriptures themselves. There are thirty-nine books that make up what we now call the Old Testament of our Bible. These books are of various types. There are five books of law, twelve books of history, five books of poetry and seventeen books of prophecy (five major prophets and twelve minor prophets). Nearly thirty writers took part in the writing of the thirty-nine books.

AN AMAZING PATTERN OF REVELATION

> Throughout the whole of the Old Testament, there is an intricately interwoven picture that cannot be mistaken for any other figure in history than He [Jesus]!

Contained within these thirty-nine books, there are more than three hundred prophecies that were directly fulfilled in the thirty-three year life span of Jesus of Nazareth. And throughout the whole of the Old Testament, there is an intricately interwoven picture that cannot be mistaken for any other figure in history than He. The proof is that those Jews who reject Jesus are yet looking for someone to come to fulfill the many prophecies of their sacred Scriptures. No one else has been able to fit the complete picture.

The possibility of thirty men, living in different cities, in different generations, with different teachers and from different backgrounds, and yet agreeing in the general theme of their books and in three hundred distinct prophetic utterances that centered on one man, is mathematically unsound. This was an astounding miraculous sign from God that Jesus was the long-waited Messiah.

Each of the three hundred prophecies were so filled with detail that the mathematical possibility of chance in their human inspiration is out of the question. We must believe what the Scriptures claim for themselves: *"Holy men of God spoke as they were moved by the Holy Spirit"* (2 Peter 1:21, NKJ).

WHAT THE SCRIPTURES MEANT TO THESE PEOPLE

It is important to note in the context of ancient Jewish society, the Scriptures were not just something that one could take or leave as it suited their fancy. Neither was it the case, as in most religions, that some few were familiar with the sacred writings and the masses were nearly or completely ignorant of them. On the contrary, every single Jewish lad was expected to begin a thorough study of the Law and the prophets beginning at an early age. Although this study of Law often had much tradition thrown in, yet the Scriptures were a requirement for every male, and these Scriptures pointed emphatically and directly to Jesus as the long-awaited Messiah.

This astounding fulfillment of Scripture was one of the major themes of the book of Matthew, and the words *"This fulfilled"* are repeated over and over again in the course of that book. For instance:

That night Joseph left for Egypt with the child and Mary, his mother, and they stayed there until Herod's death. This fulfilled what the Lord had spoken through the prophet: "I called my Son out of Egypt."   Matthew 2:14-15

67

In this passage, Matthew was referring to Hosea 11:1:

*"When Israel was a child, I loved him,
and I called my son out of Egypt."*

Keep in mind that Matthew was a Jew and his book was written to a Jewish audience. The men who confronted Jesus, demanding some miraculous sign of His authority, claimed faith in and obedience to the Jewish Scriptures. *"Hypocrites,"* said Jesus, *"an evil, adulterous generation."* How could He say that so decidedly and so emphatically? Because these men chose to willfully ignore the totality of the miraculous signs He was sending their way. They willfully and knowingly rejected His *Infallible Proofs*.

Chapter 3

Jesus' Miraculous Birth

"All right then, the Lord himself will give you the sign. Look! The virgin will conceive a child! She will give birth to a son and will call him Immanuel (which means 'God is with us')."   Isaiah 7:14

The utterly amazing details surrounding the birth of Jesus reveal many miraculous fulfillments of prophecy, and each of them became in itself, a miraculous and obvious sign to the people of His day, proving His authenticity as the Son of God. And, of course, these miraculous events still speak to us today.

The Pronouncement by the Prophet Isaiah

As a starter, some seven hundred years before Christ, the Jewish prophet Isaiah, inspired by the Holy Spirit, spoke the amazing words above. At first, when the prophet admonished King Ahaz to ask God for a sign, Ahaz refused, saying that he felt it would be tempting God to do that. It was then that Isaiah gave his famous reply, foretelling the particular part of Jesus' birth that would seem so astonishing to men and women everywhere since that time. The Messiah would be born from a virgin, a woman who had never yet had sexual relations with a man.

As we all know, such a birth would be against nature, against the natural order set in place by God Himself. It was God who ordained that a man and a woman be joined and that the result of their union would be the conception of a new life. A virgin birth, therefore, is, by definition, impossible. And yet God chose to reveal Jesus in this very unorthodox way.

Today, in the twenty-first century, we have artificial insemination that permits a single woman to become pregnant and bear a child, but the process is still the same as that established by the Creator so long ago. Human conception and birth does not take place without the union of a man's sperm and a woman's egg. This has made the idea of a virgin birth laughable to intellectuals throughout the centuries. In a moment, we'll get back to this matter of virginity and childbirth. First, let's look at the Child's name and what it means.

THE CHILD'S NAME AND WHAT IT MEANS

In his original prophetic utterance, Isaiah called the Child who would be miraculously conceived and born

Immanuel and identified that term as meaning *"God is with us."* But Immanuel (or Emmanuel as it is often written) was not meant to be the given name of the Child. Rather, as we shall see, His name was to be Jesus.

In another instance Isaiah prophesied:

"For a child is born to us,
a son is given to us.
The government will rest on his shoulders.
And he will be called:
Wonderful Counselor, Mighty God,
Everlasting Father, Prince of Peace."
                                    Isaiah 9:6

> *Human conception and birth does not take place without the union of a man's sperm and a woman's egg!*

Seven hundred years later, the angel Gabriel, a heavenly messenger, appeared to Mary, the woman who was chosen to be the Child's mother, and explained to her that she was chosen by God to bear the Messiah and that she was to call the Child *"Jesus,"* which means *"Savior"*:

God sent the angel Gabriel to Nazareth, a village in Galilee, to a virgin named Mary. She was engaged to be married to a man named Joseph, a descendant of King David. Gabriel appeared to her and

71

said, "Greetings, favored woman! The Lord is with you!"
Confused and disturbed, Mary tried to think what the
angel could mean. "Don't be afraid, Mary," the angel
told her, "for you have found favor with God! You will
conceive and give birth to a son, and you will name him
Jesus. He will be very great and will be called the Son of
the Most High. The Lord God will give him the throne of
his ancestor David. And he will reign over Israel forever;
his Kingdom will never end!" Luke 1:26-33

For names, we now have Jesus, Savior, Emmanuel
(God With Us), Wonderful Counsellor (or Wonderful,
Counselor, as many translations render it), the Mighty
God, the Everlasting Father, the Prince of Peace ... . What
was the Child's real name? His name was Jesus, but He
was to be all of the rest and more. Each of these names,
prophetically and supernaturally given, became a supernatural sign to the Jewish people of who Jesus really was
and what He had come to Earth to do.

THAT MATTER OF A VIRGIN BIRTH

So Jesus was born to a woman named Mary, a resi-
dent of Nazareth, a town situated in the Galilee (the area
between the Mediterranean Sea and the Sea of Galilee in
what is present-day Israel). She was a very young woman
(some think as young as fourteen), but she was already
engaged to Joseph, a carpenter of the same town. Most
importantly, she was still a virgin. They had not consummated their relationship sexually.

As we have noted, many mock the idea of the virgin birth as a mere fable, thinking it to be impossible, but please consider the facts in the matter. The Jewish Law was very severe in such matters, and any woman had to think twice before committing such an offense against local law and accepted social custom. The risks were simply too great. Usually a woman who was found to be pregnant out of wedlock was stoned to death.

At the very least, when an unwed woman among them was with child, everyone in the community knew it, and it was a terrible scandal. And yet was this not exactly what Isaiah had forewarned the people to look for?

"Look! The virgin will conceive a child! She will give birth to a son."

What Should Joseph Do?

Mary was not the only one affected by this situation. There was her fiancé, Joseph, to consider. If you had been Joseph, what would you have thought? The sweet, pure, innocent country girl that he was engaged to marry came to him one day, asking him to be understanding because she had seen an angel who told her that she would become pregnant and give birth to a child.

This put Joseph in a very difficult position. He had entered into a binding espousal contract with this woman, and, although they were not yet living together, he was already considered to be her *"husband"* (Matthew 1:19, KJV).

He could not lawfully break this engagement, so just what were his options?

> **If he exposed the woman, he would then be free to marry another, but Mary might be put to death for her "crime"!**

If he exposed the woman, he would then be free to marry another, but Mary might be put to death for her "crime." According to the Law, he could also consummate the marriage and then bring charges of impurity against her. The Law was quite lenient in this way, giving all the rights to the man:

"Suppose a man marries a woman but she does not please him. Having discovered something wrong with her, he writes her a letter of divorce, hands it to her, and sends her away from his house."

Deuteronomy 24:1

Two factors prevented Joseph from taking either of these steps. First, he loved Mary, and he did not want to hurt her (even though he now thought she had been unfaithful to him). Second, any charge of infidelity he made against Mary would implicate him as well, for he would naturally be suspected as having fathered the illicit child.

What Joseph feared most was that Mary would be subjected to public ridicule. He loved her too much to see her endure that. Matthew recorded his decided response in this way:

Joseph, her fiancé, was a good man and did not want to disgrace her publicly, so he decided to break the engagement quietly. Matthew 1:19

Joseph was *"a good man."* The King James Version of the Bible uses the phrase "a *just man.*" It was not only Mary who had been chosen by God. Both she and Joseph were chosen for their assigned roles in this matter. Mary must give birth to the Child, the Savior of all mankind, but Joseph must serve as His earthly guardian until He was grown. Her husband, therefore, must be wise and just, *"a good man,"* and Joseph fit the bill.

A MIRACULOUS INTERVENTION

Being the good man that he was, Joseph was not willing to make Mary a public example, to *"disgrace her publicly."* His decision, therefore, was to *"break the engagement quietly"* or, as the King James Version of the Bible puts it, *"put her away privily."* Some have taken this to mean that he intended to send her away secretly. But then, another miraculous occurrence intervened:

But while he thought on these things, behold, the angel of the LORD appeared unto him in a dream, saying, Joseph, thou son of David, fear not to take unto thee Mary thy wife: for that which is conceived in her is of the Holy Ghost. And she shall bring forth a son, and thou shalt call his name Jesus: for he shall save his people from their sins. Matthew 1:20-21

This was basically the same thing that had happened to Mary. Was it the very same angel who had spoken to her? Perhaps. What is important is that Joseph believed and obeyed the message of the angel. God knew that he would, and that's why He had chosen Joseph in the first place. Joseph now took the legal step of taking Mary as his wife and, thus, affording her his covering.

THE DELICACY OF THEIR CIRCUMSTANCES

This was a very delicate step and must have produced moments of discomfort for both of them. As legally joined husband and wife, they now had all the rights of conjugal living. They loved each other, and would have been naturally attracted to each other sexually. But, because of all that had happened, Mary knew that their union could not be consummated just yet, and Joseph knew it too:

When Joseph woke up, he did as the angel of the Lord commanded and took Mary as his wife. But he did not have sexual relations with her until her son was born. And Joseph named him Jesus. Matthew 1:24-25

This is another proof of the fact that Joseph was indeed *"a good man."* Who would have known if they had consum-

76

mated their relationship? And who could have complained about it? They were, after all, married. But just as they were the only ones who knew about the visitation of the angelic messenger, they were the ones God was intrusting to bring Jesus into the world through a miracle. Therefore, Joseph was careful not to begin their sexual relationship until after the Child was born. He was to be born of a virgin.

PREPARATIONS FOR A MIRACULOUS BIRTH

In this way, the preparations were made for a miraculous birth. Angels paved the way. The Holy Spirit planted the seed of God in the womb of a righteous woman, and that seed grew to produce the God-Child Jesus. He was to became totally God and totally man, something never before heard of (except in mythology). It was all so that He could be our Savior, our Wonderful Counselor, our Mighty God, our Everlasting Father, our Prince of Peace.

As a footnote to this sacred union, the lineage (family line) of both Mary and Joseph, the mother and step-father of Jesus, was a fulfillment of prophecy:

The Lord swore an oath to David
with a promise he will never take back:
"I will place one of your descendants
on your throne."   Psalm 132:11

Out of the stump of David's family will grow a shoot —
yes, a new Branch bearing fruit from the old root.
                                      Isaiah 11:1

This was all part of the many *Infallible Proofs* God presented to His people and which most would willfully and knowingly reject. How blind!

CHAPTER 4

AN ANGELIC VISITATION

That night there were shepherds staying in the fields nearby, guarding their flocks of sheep. Suddenly, an angel of the Lord appeared among them, and the radiance of the Lord's glory surrounded them. They were terrified.

Luke 2:8-9

On the very night when Jesus was born in Bethlehem, there was a strange happening on a nearby hillside. Shepherds were guarding their flocks, when suddenly an intense light shone upon them: *"The radiance of the Lord's glory surrounded them."* They were very frightened by this phenomenon.

DO NOT BE AFRAID

When they could look, the shepherds saw an angel, and that angel spoke to them these powerful words:

"Do not be afraid, for behold, I bring you good tidings of great joy which will be to all people. For there is born to you this day in the city of David a Savior, who is Christ the Lord. And this will be the sign to you: You will find a Babe wrapped in swaddling cloths, lying in a manger."

Luke 2:10-12, NKJ

> As if this was not enough, suddenly there appeared with the first angel a whole multitude of heavenly beings, all speaking in unison!

As if this was not enough, suddenly there appeared with the first angel a whole multitude of heavenly beings, all speaking in unison and saying:

"Glory to God in the highest, and on Earth peace, good will toward men." Luke 2:14, NKJ

What a dynamic experience! Angels, described in the New Living Version of the Bible as *"the armies of heaven,"* appeared to humble shepherds. And what these angels said was the most thrilling part. Their good news, they said, was for *"all people."* A Savior had been born, and that Savior was *"Christ the Lord."*

Christ is the Greek form of the word "Messiah," and because of the Greek influence in the Roman Empire, the term *Christ* became commonly used to speak of the coming Deliverer. Now the angels declared that Jesus was this *"Christ,"* the long-awaited Messiah. He for whom they had waited so long had finally come.

Could It Be True?

Could it be true? It must have been very difficult for the shepherds to believe, for the angel said that a sign would be given to them to prove the truth of the message. But what a strange sign! They would find the Baby Christ, the angel said, wrapped in swaddling clothes (grave clothes) and lying in a manger (a feeding trough for cattle).

The New Living Translation of the Bible simply calls these swaddling clothes *"strips of cloth"* (Luke 2:12). The people of that area wrapped their dead in linen cloth that was wound in narrow rolls. After one wrapping, they placed preserving spices, then wrapped another layer, and continued this process as they were able. The more wrappings and spices they could afford, the better preserved the body of a loved one would be, and the longer it would last without decaying.

But how strange to find a newborn baby wrapped in grave clothes and lying, of all places, in a feeding trough for cattle! And yet that was the sign the angel gave them. If shepherds wanted to invent a fancy story to pass the hours of the lonely night, they surely could have done better. Who would believe a God-Child in grave clothes lying in a manger? But this story did not come from shepherds. It came from angels, heavenly messengers.

OVERWHELMED BY IT ALL

The shepherds were overwhelmed by it all, but they could not doubt what had been spoken to them. So they left their sheep and went into the town in search of the Christ Child. They did not look in the mayor's house, nor in any house, for that matter. They searched where the angel had instructed them—in the stables. In a stable behind a local inn, they found Mary and Joseph and the Babe, whom Mary had laid on the straw of a manger. And how do you suppose the newborn Child was clothed? Yes! He was wrapped with grave clothes, just as the angel had said.

What a coincidence—that ignorant shepherds would know the details of such an unorthodox birth! Is this just a ridiculous myth? Why would any mother or father in their right mind wrap a child in grave cloth and lay it in a manager?

THE TRUTH OF THE STORY

The truth of the story is this: Mary and Joseph had been compelled to make a journey to Bethlehem from their home in Nazareth, to register for a tax which the Roman ruler, Caesar Augustus, had imposed on his entire empire. Since they were of the house and lineage of David, they must register in the city of David, Bethlehem. In actuality, Bethlehem was not much of a city, but it had been called the city of David since the time of King David, ten centuries before Christ.

The journey from Nazareth to Bethlehem apparently took longer than expected, and Mary was ready for delivery when they reached the city. Because of the crowd of taxpayers, however, the inns were full. Joseph searched, but found no decent place of refuge for his young wife. The only vacancy was in a stable, so Mary and Joseph took refuge in a stable, and a King was born that night in a cattle stall. It was clean and warm, but very humble—a fitting beginning for a life such as this Man would live.

Mary and Joseph had no blanket for Jesus, but someone brought some clean linen cloth. No matter that it was grave cloth; it would keep the Child warm; so they wrapped Him in it.

Then, there was the problem of a bed. Someone filled a manger with soft hay, and thus made a bed for a King. And in this way, the Savior of the world was born.

Angels heralded the news to simple shepherds on a hillside, for the Pharisees, in their golden robes, could hardly fathom a king in swaddling clothes. The shepherds had now come and found that it was all true, as strange as it may have seemed to them and to others.

What Did the Shepherds Do Next?

What did the shepherds do next?

After seeing him, the shepherds told everyone what had happened and what the angel had said to them about this child. Luke 2:17

They *"told everyone."* The King James Version of the Bible says it this way:

And when they had seen it, they made known abroad the saying which was told them concerning this Child.

Similarly, the New King James Version uses the phrase *"they made widely known the saying."* The shepherds couldn't keep silent about these wonderful events. They had to tell others. Just imagine their excitement, as they related the strange chain of events over and over again to anyone willing to listen.

It's very possible that the shepherds went about the town, pounding on doors, rousing people from their sleep to hear the story. They *"made widely known the saying"* of the angels. They talked about it so much that it became a familiar tale, and not just in Bethlehem. The term the King James Version uses, again, is this: *"They made known abroad the saying."* You can be sure that Jerusalem, only a few miles away, heard about what had happened that night in Bethlehem, and you can be sure that the religious leaders who made Jerusalem their home heard about it too.

What Was the Reaction of Those Who Heard It?

What was the reaction of those who heard it?
All who heard the shepherds' story were astonished.
Luke 2:18

"Astonished?" So did they run to the stable to find Jesus for themselves? There is no record that they did. Did they perhaps invite the Holy Family into their homes? Again, there is no record of it. In fact, the King James and New King James Versions of the Bible use a far less excited word than astonished to describe the reaction of the people who heard the testimony of the shepherds. They say simply:

They "wondered," but did they accept Him for who He really was?

And all they that heard it wondered at those things which were told them by the shepherds.

They *"wondered,"* but did they believe? They *"wondered,"* but did they accept Him for who He really was? There no indication of it.

The shepherds were excited, and they *"told everyone what had happened and what the angel had said to them about this child,"* but the reaction was not what we might have expected. Others were very slow to receive

85

a God/King born in a stable, wrapped in grave clothes and placed in a feeding trough.

NOT DISCOURAGED

This apparent lack of enthusiasm on the part of those who heard the strange tale did not discourage the shepherds at all. They knew what they had seen and heard. For the rest of their lives, no doubt, they frequently spoke with fervor of the events of that strange night. The Scripture conclude their portion of the story with these telling words:

The shepherds went back to their flocks, glorifying and praising God for all they had heard and seen. It was just as the angel had told them.   Luke 2:20

Everything had been just *"as the angel had told them,"* and they would never forget it—whatever others chose to do.

The very night Jesus was born God raised up witnesses from the Judean hills and sent them everywhere proclaiming the message of the angels and the fulfillment discovered on a bed of straw; but the hearers only wondered. There is no record of others visiting the stable, no others who glorified and praised God, no others who bore forth the glad tidings—only wonder. Wonder, but not acceptance. Wonder, but not belief.

God's people expected and waited patiently for a powerful king who would lead great armies, deliver them from all their enemies, and make them a great nation. They had no time for a manger King! The fact that angels declared the events of that night upon a Judean hillside meant little to them. They willfully and knowingly rejected God's many *Infallible Proofs*.

CHAPTER 5

MIRACULOUS SIGNS
IN THE HEAVENS

Jesus was born in Bethlehem in Judea, during the reign of King Herod. About that time some wise men from eastern lands arrived in Jerusalem, asking, "Where is the newborn king of the Jews? We saw his star as it rose, and we have come to worship him."   Matthew 2:1-2

The very heavens declared the birth of the Christ Child. Astrologers in various parts of the inhabited world noticed a strange star appearing in the eastern section of the heavens. The Bible records the fact that several men, having seen the star, set out on a journey to Judea that took somewhere around two years to complete.

We are not told the number, the names, or the nationality of the men. Tradition sets the number at three, probably because there were three gifts presented to the Christ Child. We cannot say for sure how many there were. Some have called the men "magi" or kings. The Bible simply describes them as *"wise men from eastern lands."* And any idea about where they might have come from is also speculation.

India and China especially have long believed in the signs of the heavens. Persia (modern-day Iran) had men similar to those described in the Bible. Maybe these men were Indians or Chinese or Persians. We cannot say for sure. What we can say for sure is that the wise men traveled a long way and would not have done it for little or no reason. They were sure of what the signs of the heavens were telling them. What they saw was so unusual that it caused them to leave their homeland and take a very long, uncertain, and dangerous journey to find the Christ Child.

WHAT EXACTLY DID THEY SEE?

What exactly did these men see that had such an impact upon them? So far no one knows for sure. Some scientists have proposed the theory that the men saw a meteor, which came near Earth and then burned up and disintegrated in the atmosphere.

Another theory, derived from astronomical calculations, is that around the year 7 B.C. the path of the three planets, Saturn, Jupiter and Venus, as seen from Earth, came so close together that they appeared to be one great star. Since our calenders have changed several times over the years, it now seems that Jesus was born in either 4 or 5 B.C. And since the star which the wise men saw appeared two years earlier, this may have been the phenomenon which they witnessed.

If so, it only proves the supernatural aspect of this sign, for such a uniting of the planets rarely lasts for more than a few days, and yet the star which the wise men saw reappeared nearly two years later over Jerusalem, moved on to Bethlehem and stood still over the house where Jesus was staying. This was not a natural occurrence. This was a miraculous sign from Heaven.

WHAT DID THE STAR MEAN?

We cannot be sure that these united planets formed the mysterious star which the Asian astrologers saw. We don't know. We do know they saw a star, that star steered a strange course, and they followed it for two years. They would only have done this if they were con-

What we can say for sure is that the wise men traveled a long way and would not have done it for little or no reason!

vinced that the appearance of the star signified a major event in history.

Their journey eventually brought them to Jerusalem, and there they inquired about the Child:

"Where is the newborn king of the Jews? We saw his star as it rose, and we have come to worship him."

Matthew 2:2

Why would men of other countries travel so far just to worship the *"king of the Jews?"* What made them interested in a foreign king anyway? The kingdom of the Jews was not large. In fact, it was fairly insignificant as kingdoms went in those days. Because of this, it seems clear to me that the message of the heavens the astrologers witnessed agreed with the message of the angels who had appeared at the time of Jesus' birth. This good news was to be to *"all people"* (Luke 2:10). Jesus was to be the Savior, not only of the Jews, but also of the Indians, the Chinese, the Persians, the Asians, the Africans, the Europeans, the Americans and everyone else on planet Earth. The heavens declared it, and the wise men believed it so firmly that they went in search of Him.

WHERE WAS HE?

When the wise men made their stop at Jerusalem, they requested an audience with the current king, Herod the Great. This shows us that these men were wealthy and respected and accustomed to dealing with those of high estate. However, the news they brought so disturbed

Herod and he raised such a fuss over it that all Jerusalem heard about the matter.

It may be understandable that Herod was troubled by such news. After all, this was a man who murdered several of his own sons and, eventually, his favorite wife, Mariamne, because of their imagined attempts to take his throne from him. He could not stand the thought of a king whom the heavens declared and whom strangers from afar were coming to honor. What is fairly surprising, however, is that the people of Jerusalem were also said to be troubled by the news the wise men brought:

> *King Herod was deeply disturbed when he heard this, as was everyone in Jerusalem.*   Matthew 2:3

Who was disturbed? *"Everyone in Jerusalem."* Can there be any doubt that the religious leaders, who worked and made their home in that city, would know about three strangers who had appeared at the palace asking for an audience with the king to inquire about a Child-King? There can be no doubt. God did not do these things in a corner. He declared them on the housetops so that none would be ignorant of them. In fact, the Chief Priests and scribes were called into the middle of this whole affair.

HEROD WAS TROUBLED

For some time, Herod had been hearing other troubling rumors about the birth of a Child King, so now he gathered all the Chief Priests and scribes together and asked them where the expected Messiah would be born.

> *For some time, Herod had been hearing other troubling rumors about the birth of a Child King!*

Now, think about that for a moment. How would these men be expected to know where the Messiah would be born? The answer is surprisingly simple. The Scriptures declared exactly where the Messiah would be born. After consulting among themselves, the priests and scribes answered Herod without fear of error:

"In Bethlehem in Judea," they said, "for this is what the prophet wrote:

*'And you, O Bethlehem in the land of Judah,
are not least among the ruling cities of Judah,
for a ruler will come from you
who will be the shepherd for my people Israel.' "*   Matthew 2:5-6

These men were quoting from their own sacred Scriptures:

*"But you, O Bethlehem Ephrathah,
are only a small village among all the people of Judah.
Yet a ruler of Israel will come from you,
one whose origins are from the distant past."*   Micah 5:2

When Herod heard these things, he called the men from the East again and asked them when they had first seen the star. They answered that it had first appeared nearly two years before. Herod may have feigned otherwise, but he took this all very seriously. He was convinced that this was no "old-wives fable" and that his throne was in immediate danger. The proof is that he decided to take desperate measures to preserve his future. He must find this Child and kill Him. Nothing else would do.

Herod told the wise men to go to Bethlehem and find the Child and then return and tell him where the Babe was, so that he might go and worship Him also. This talk of Herod worshiping the Child, of course, was a pretense. The sooner he could find Jesus the sooner he could eliminate this perceived threat to his throne.

THE STAR ACTUALLY GUIDED THEM

The wise men started off toward Bethlehem, and the star they had seen in the East reappeared and went before them, until it stood over the place where the Child was:

After this interview the wise men went their way. And the star they had seen in the east guided them to Bethlehem. It went ahead of them and stopped over the place where the child was.   Matthew 2:9

Today we have GPS (Global Positioning Satellite) technology that enables us to chart our exact location and head in any desired direction, but in the time of

Herod and Jesus such a thing was scientifically impossible. Instead, God did something so supernatural that no one could doubt it. The same star the wise men had been following now for nearly two years went before them, guiding them, until it came to the exact spot where the Child was. Then, it stopped moving and stood still in the sky. Again, what kind of star could do that? This was nothing short of miraculous, and everyone knew it.

DID THE STAR LEAD THEM TO THE STABLE?

Did the star lead the wise men to the stable? Our popular cultural understanding of the Christmas story has them there, standing or kneeling behind Mary and Joseph, but the Scriptures paint a very different picture. Two years had passed since Jesus was born in a stable, so Joseph and Mary were no longer in such a place.

They were still in Bethlehem. The Lord had shown Joseph that it would be dangerous just then to take Jesus home to Nazareth, so the family was now living in a house in Bethlehem. When the star came to rest, it stood over that very house:

They entered the house and saw the child with his mother, Mary, and they bowed down and worshiped him. Then they opened their treasure chests and gave him gifts of gold, frankincense, and myrrh. Matthew 2:11

These men had journeyed for two years and spent a huge sum of money, all to be able to see the Child whom the heavens declared as the coming king. But it was not enough that they had expended precious time and money; they wanted to do more. They fell down and worshiped Him, knowing instinctively that He was not just another human being and that He was worthy of their adoration.

THE GIFTS

Then they went even further. It was not enough to seek Him out and worship Him; they wanted to give Him gifts, expensive gifts. It has been said that no one could have brought anything more valuable in that day. Gold has always been a valued commodity, giving rise to our common saying, "It's worth its weight in gold." It was in the search of gold that many of the conquistadores set forth on their long and dangerous voyages. In this case, the matter was reversed. These men did not come in search of gold; they came bearing gold as a gift to Him who would be Savior of the world.

Their second gift was frankincense, one of the rarest of aromatic resins. It has been traded in the Middle East and North Africa for thousands of years.

The third gift was myrrh, another rare resin, this one valued for its use in preserving the bodies of the dead. This is very significant. First, Jesus was wrapped in grave clothes moments after He was born into this world, and then men from afar came bearing a gift of myrrh for Him. These were signs that He had been born to die for all mankind.

These valuable gifts, brought so humbly by noble and wise men, no doubt represented God's means of sustaining His Son and His guardians (Mary and Joseph) during the flight into Egypt which would soon follow.

HEROD'S RAGE

We are not told how long the wise men stayed in Bethlehem. We are told, however, that while they were in that place, God spoke to one of them in a dream and told him that Herod actually wanted to kill the Child, so they should not return to him as planned. Would they risk offending such an important king? Yes, for they now worshipped a greater King. It was for this reason that they chose another route when they eventually departed for their own country, bypassing Jerusalem and avoiding Herod.

When Herod saw that he had been deceived, he was furious. His rage drove him to put into operation an even more wicked and desperate plan. He sent soldiers throughout Bethlehem and the surrounding area with the order to kill all the children two years old and under. This would surely take care of the miraculous Child, born some two years before. The plan failed only because Joseph was warned by the angel of the Lord in a dream. He got up immediately and fled by night to Egypt with Mary and Jesus, and they remained there until Herod died:

> *After the wise men were gone, an angel of the Lord appeared to Joseph in a dream. "Get up! Flee to Egypt with the child and his mother," the angel said. "Stay there until*

I tell you to return, because Herod is going to search for the child to kill him."
That night Joseph left for Egypt with the child and Mary, his mother, and they stayed there until Herod's death.
Matthew 2:13-15

Thank God for this sensitive and obedient man who willingly took on the dangerous and heavy responsibility of protecting the life of the Child he knew had been born to save all mankind.

The slaying of the Judean children was prophesied by Jeremiah six hundred years before the birth of Christ:

This is what the Lord says:
"A cry is heard in Ramah—
deep anguish and bitter weeping.
Rachel weeps for her children,
refusing to be comforted—
for her children are gone."
Jeremiah 31:15

> *He [Joseph] got up immediately and fled by night to Egypt with Mary and Jesus!*

The flight into Egypt was prophesied by Hosea seven hundred and forty years before the birth of Christ and by Baalam fourteen hundred years before the birth of Christ:

99

*"When Israel was a child, I loved him,
and I called my son out of Egypt."*   Hosea 11:1

*"God brought them out of Egypt;
for them he is as strong as a wild ox.
He devours all the nations that oppose him,
breaking their bones in pieces,
shooting them with arrows."*   Numbers 24:8

So many miraculous signs! Why did men willfully and knowingly chose to deny these *Infallible Proofs?*

CHAPTER 6

MIRACULOUS CONFIRMATIONS IN THE TEMPLE

Eight days later, when the baby was circumcised, he was named Jesus, the name given him by the angel even before he was conceived. Then it was time for their purification offering, as required by the law of Moses after the birth of a child; so his parents took him to Jerusalem to present him to the Lord. Luke 2:21-22

Although Herod didn't seem to be aware of it, Jesus had already been right there in Jerusalem, brought to the Temple soon after His birth by his parents for an important Jewish religious ceremony.

THE CIRCUMSTANCES OF THEIR VISIT

It was the duty of every conscientious Jewish couple, whose first child was male, to present that child to the Lord in the Temple at Jerusalem and offer the sacrifices designated by sacred law:

> *While they [Mary and Joseph] were there in the Temple that day some very strange things happened!*

"Dedicate to me every firstborn among the Israelites. The first off-spring to be born, of both humans and animals, belongs to me."
                                                    Exodus 13:2

"You must not hold anything back when you give me offerings from your crops and your wine.
"You must give me your firstborn sons."   Exodus 22:29

"Look, I have chosen the Levites from among the Israelites to serve as substitutes for all the firstborn sons of the people of Israel. The Levites belong to me, for all the firstborn males are mine. On the day I struck down all the firstborn sons of the Egyptians, I set apart for myself all the firstborn in Israel, both of people and of animals. They are mine; I am the Lord."   Numbers 3:12-13

Joseph and Mary, a most devout couple, made the short trip from Bethlehem to Jerusalem in obedience to these sacred commands, and while they were there in the Temple that day some very strange things happened.

WHO WAS SIMEON?

There was an old man by the name of Simeon living in Jerusalem who was recognized by those who knew him as a just (righteous) and devout person, one anointed with the Holy Spirit. This man firmly believed that God had given him a personal message that he would not die before he had seen the promised Messiah:

At that time there was a man in Jerusalem named Simeon. He was righteous and devout and was eagerly waiting for the Messiah to come and rescue Israel. The Holy Spirit was upon him and had revealed to him that he would not die until he had seen the Lord's Messiah. Luke 2:25-26

Even as he continued to age, Simeon waited with great expectation for all of this to happen, as he was sure it would. God has spoken it, and He would not fail.

Because of his position as a spiritual father in Israel, you can be sure that this man Simeon was well known by the people of the city, and when anyone from inside or outside of the city visited the Temple, they found Simeon there praying and worshiping. He was highly respected by his fellow men.

Simeon's Miraculous Response
to the Presence of Jesus

On the very day that Joseph and Mary arrived at Jerusalem, and just a little while before they went into the Temple, the Spirit of God also led Simeon to come there. When the parents brought in the Child Jesus, Simeon was there waiting, and he was immediately and miraculously drawn to the Child:

> Simeon was there. He took the child in his arms and praised God, saying,
> "Sovereign Lord, now let your servant die in peace,
> as you have promised.
> I have seen your salvation,
> which you have prepared for all people.
> He is a light to reveal God to the nations,
> and he is the glory of your people Israel!"
>
> Luke 2:28-32

How strange that a man would walk up to a visiting couple, and, without a word, take their child into his arms! And how strange that a mother and father would willingly give their child into the arms of someone they have never met and don't know! Simeon was being led by the Spirit, and so were Mary and Joseph.

Simeon then turned to Mary, who was overwhelmed by the words she had just heard him utter, and he spoke directly to her:

"This child is destined to cause many in Israel to fall, but he will be a joy to many others. He has been sent as a sign from God, but many will oppose him."   Luke 2:34

As accustomed as Joseph and Mary were by now to the miracles of God and the miraculous words that accompanied them, they were both thrilled and amazed by this unusual, supernatural confirmation from Heaven. The Scriptures record:

Jesus' parents were amazed at what was being said about him.   Luke 2:33

Part of what Simeon said that day was intended for everyone to hear and understand, but the part he spoke to Mary was specifically for her and Joseph. Many would oppose Jesus, and this man and woman were commissioned by God to protect Him until He was capable of protecting Himself.

WHAT DID IT ALL MEAN?

What Simeon said revealed what it all meant. He was convinced that he was now ready to die, for he had seen the Lord's Christ:

"Sovereign Lord, now let your servant die in peace,
as you have promised.
"I have seen your salvation."

As a respected figure in the Jewish community and in their most sacred Temple, he was confirming that Jesus was indeed the promised Messiah. What a powerful and convincing sign!

WHO WAS ANNA?

If these happenings were not enough to point to Jesus as the Messiah, another strange thing took place that same day. There was an elderly widow in the Temple, a prophetess, whose name was Anna.

Anna's husband had died after seven years of marriage, and instead of remarrying, as most Jewish widows did, she chose to enter the Temple and remain there night and day, serving God with fasting and prayer. She was now eighty-four years old, so she had been doing this for a very long time:

Anna, a prophet, was also there in the Temple. She was the daughter of Phanuel from the tribe of Asher, and she was very old. Her husband died when they had been married only seven years. Then she lived as a widow to the age of eighty-four. She never left the Temple but stayed there day and night, worshiping God with fasting and prayer.

Luke 2:36-37

The Jerusalem Temple was the focal point of daily life in Israel. No matter where Jews lived (the Jewish population was quite spread out), they must spend a certain amount of time in the Temple each year. Those who lived nearby went there every day for worship and learning. Those who lived farther away went on special occasions. Those special occasions included the yearly sacrifice for sins, the feasts (Passover, Pentecost, Trumpets, Tabernacles, Purim, Dedication or Lights, etc.), the birth of the first male child, certain diseases that required cleansing ceremonies, and any other situation that required animal sacrifice.

Every conscientious and devout Jewish family visited the Jerusalem Temple at least yearly, and when they did visit the Temple, they met a woman who had been prophesying there for many years. Would it be wrong to suppose that all the devout Jews knew Anna well? In my way of thinking, there can be no doubt about it. Even the children knew Old Anna.

No matter where Jews lived they must spend a certain amount of time in the Temple each year!

On that Very Day and at that Precise Moment

Now, on the particular day that Joseph and Mary visited the Temple and at the very instant that Simeon ended his message to Mary, Anna came to that part of the Temple and worshiped Jesus also, giving thanks to God that at last her prayers were answered—the Savior was born. How amazing! Without a word from Simeon about the revelation God had given him, Anna also immediately recognized Jesus as the Messiah.

> *She came along just as Simeon was talking with Mary and Joseph, and she began praising God.* Luke 2:38

What the Bible says next about Anna is the most important part of all:

> *She talked about the child to everyone who had been waiting expectantly for God to rescue Jerusalem.*
> Luke 2:38

The New King James Bible says it this way:

> *She gave thanks to the Lord, and spoke of Him to all those who looked for redemption in Jerusalem.*

Anna had been in the Temple long enough to know those who truly believed that one day the Messiah would come—those who *"looked for redemption," "who had been waiting expectantly for God to rescue Jerusalem,"* and in the days to come, she did not fail to tell even one of them about the Child Jesus. How phenomenal!

SIGN UPON SIGN

The angels declared the birth of a Savior, and the shepherds forwarded that message to many at home and *"abroad."* The heavens declared the birth of a Savior, and the wise men forwarded that message to many, including King Herod the Great and the entire city of Jerusalem. The Spirit of God declared the birth of a Savior, and Simeon and Anna forwarded that message to *"all who looked for redemption."* Could it be that the scribes and Pharisees were not among those who sincerely *"looked for redemption"*? Could it be that they were too proud, heady and high-minded, to learn from humble shepherds, foreign astrologers, or an elderly widow?

How right Jesus was when He called these men *"hypocrites."* Only *"an evil, adulterous generation"* could have failed to recognize and believe all the many miraculous signs that God was giving them. They willingly and knowingly ignored His *Infallible Proofs.*

CHAPTER 7

JESUS' MIRACULOUS CHILDHOOD

When Jesus' parents had fulfilled all the requirements of the law of the Lord, they returned home to Nazareth in Galilee. There the child grew up healthy and strong. He was filled with wisdom, and God's favor was on him.

Luke 2:39-40

We know very little about the growing-up period of Jesus' life. What little we do know, however, is significant and worthy of our attention. This passage, although it is a very short glimpse at His early life, denotes three miraculous things about the young child Jesus.

HE WAS "STRONG IN SPIRIT"

The New Living Translation says simply that Jesus grew up healthy and strong. The King James and New King James Versions, however, render this phrase a little different:

And the Child grew and became strong in spirit.   NKJ

"Strong in spirit" … Is this a phrase we commonly use in regards to a child? Clearly not. And what does it mean? It means that Jesus was a serious-minded boy, not prone to foolishness and childishness. How unusual!

"HE WAS FILLED WITH WISDOM"

The second miraculous sign from Jesus' childhood is that *"He was filled with wisdom."* Again, this is not a phrase we common use or hear used about a child. Children are not filled with wisdom, but Jesus was. He possessed unique wisdom for His age. How unusual!

HE WAS BLESSED BY GOD'S GRACE

The third miraculous sign that appeared in Jesus' childhood was that He was blessed by God's grace. The New Living Translation states simply that *"God's favor was on him."* The King James and New King James Versions use this terminology: *"The grace of God was upon him."*

This word *grace* means "God's unmerited favor," and is used in connection with sin. It is God's grace that enables one to overcome temptation and deny sin its pleasures. The Scriptures state:

For there is no difference; for all have sinned and fall short of the glory of God, being justified [freed from guilt] *freely by His grace through the redemption that is in Christ Jesus.* Romans 3:24

"Strong in spirit:" is this a phrase we commonly use in regards to a child? Clearly not!

The word *grace* in this passage is translated as *"undeserved kindness"* in the New Living Translation:

Yet God, with undeserved kindness, declares that we are righteous. He did this through Christ Jesus when he freed us from the penalty for our sins.

Paul taught more about this matter of grace, the *"undeserved kindness"* of God, in his letters to the churches:

"Because of his grace he declared us righteous and gave us confidence that we will inherit eternal life." Titus 3:7

"God's law was given so that all people could see how sinful they were. But as people sinned more and more, God's wonderful grace [His power to overcome sin] *became more abundant."*   Romans 5:20

Even though we were dead because of our sins, he gave us life when he raised Christ from the dead. (It is only by God's grace that you have been saved [from the punishment for sin]*!)*   Ephesians 2:5

God saved you by his grace when you believed. And you can't take credit for this; it is a gift from God.
                    Ephesians 2:8

For the grace of God has been revealed, bringing salvation [deliverance from sin] *to all people.*   Titus 2:11

So what does *"The grace of God was on Him"* mean? It means that there was an unusual sinlessness about this Boy, Jesus of Nazareth. Normal boys lie, cheat, steal and speak hatefully, but Jesus did none of these things. He was a model child. No historian has been able to point at Jesus and name any sin that He committed. NONE! EVER! How phenomenal is that?

THE ONE RECORDED EVENT IN JESUS' CHILDHOOD

Amazingly, there is only one event recorded from Jesus' childhood, but that one recorded event reveals all three of these miraculous signs that He was the anointed

Son of God. It happened in the following way: The family of Jesus traveled every year to Jerusalem to attend
the Feast of Passover. They went accompanied by a large
group of relatives and acquaintances from their home
area. On this occasion (when Jesus was twelve years old),
they had a very strange experience.

> *Every year Jesus' parents went to Jerusalem for the Pass-*
> *over festival. When Jesus was twelve years old, they at-*
> *tended the festival as usual. After the celebration was over,*
> *they started home to Nazareth, but Jesus stayed behind in*
> *Jerusalem. His parents didn't miss him at first, because*
> *they assumed he was among the other travelers. But when*
> *he didn't show up that evening, they started looking for*
> *him among their relatives and friends.* Luke 2:41-44

When the feast days had ended, Mary and Joseph departed for home. Jesus was not in sight, but they didn't
give it a second thought. He was a totally responsible
child. He would never get into trouble or become lost.
They were sure of it. They traveled all day without seeing
Him, but that fact didn't unduly concern them.

Then, when it had become too dark to travel further,
the entire company stopped for the night, but Jesus was
still not in sight. It was only then that His parents became
concerned. This was so unlike Jesus, for He had never
given them cause for worry. Maybe some harm had come
to Him. After all, when He was still just a baby, attempts
had been made on His life, and Simeon had warned them
prophetically in the Temple on the day of His dedication:

"Many will oppose him." How terrible it would be if they failed to protect this miracle Child! Mary and Joseph now began searching through the large company of traveling companions, but it was to no avail. Jesus was not among them.

When this fact became apparent, Mary and Joseph turned back to Jerusalem in their search. The Scriptures declare:

> *The Temple, obviously, was one of the last places they thought to look for the Child!*

When they couldn't find him, they went back to Jerusalem to search for him there. Three days later they finally discovered him in the Temple, sitting among the religious teachers, listening to them and asking questions. All who heard him were amazed at his understanding and his answers. Luke 2:45-47

THREE AGONIZING DAYS

It didn't take three days for Mary and Joseph to get back to Jerusalem. They had gone only *"a day's journey"* (KJV) or until the first evening. Therefore they must have spent much of the three days searching around Jerusalem itself. The Temple, obviously, was one of the last places they thought to look for the Child. Why was that? Was it because no one would have expected a twelve-year-old to be in such a place? And yet that was where the search ended after three days.

By the end of three days, Mary and Joseph must have been beside themselves with grief. They were among the few who knew exactly who Jesus was and why He had come into this world, and now they had apparently failed in their paternal duties and allowed some harm to come to Him. Sleepless and exhausted, they must have driven themselves on with their search.

When they had finally found Jesus and Mary questioned Him about why He had done this and caused them such sorrow, His reply was simply:

"But why did you need to search?" he asked. "Didn't you know that I must be in my Father's house?"
Luke 2:49

Jesus' only reaction seemed to be surprise and disappointment that His parents had worried about Him. They should have known that He could take care of Himself and that if He stayed behind in Jerusalem, it was for a good reason. But Joseph and Mary were only human and had been, no doubt, pressured by accusing relatives and friends, who may have sharply rebuked them for being so careless with one of their children—the eldest son. Whatever the cause of their anxiety, however, Jesus felt that they should have known better.

NOTICE AGAIN THE THREE MIRACULOUS CHARACTERISTICS OF THE CHILD JESUS

Notice again the three miraculous characteristics of the Child Jesus: He was not found jumping on a garbage heap, throwing stones into a pool, or watching the animals at the sheep market. Rather He was sitting in the Temple, taking an active part in the discussion of religious matters. The wisdom with which He expressed His thoughts astonished *"all who heard Him."* And He was not hateful to His mother and stepfather. Instead, the Scriptures show:

> *Then he returned to Nazareth with them and was obedient to them.* Luke 2:51

He could have insisted on remaining in Jerusalem, saying that He didn't need earthly parents, that He was able to take care of Himself. But He didn't do that. His time had not yet come. His earthly ministry had not yet started. He had more growing to do, and now He did that, again in a miraculous way:

> *Jesus grew in wisdom and in stature and in favor with God and all the people.* Luke 2:52

There are, among the apocryphal books, other accounts of miracles being done by the Child Jesus. One such account has Him forming a bird from clay at play and then throwing it into the air, only to see it fly away. Our Bible contains only this one story, a twelve-year old in Jerusalem consulting with the doctors of the Law. It is only a glimpse at Jesus' childhood, but it is a revealing glimpse, full of signs from Heaven. You can be sure that those doctors of the Law never forgot the name Jesus. They would see Him again years later.

What about the scribes and Pharisees? Did they not hear about the Child who answered difficult questions with amazing wisdom and carried a visible grace or favor of God upon Him? Surely this is the reason Jesus called them an evil, adulterous generation. They had seen so many signs, and yet they willingly and knowingly chose to reject God's *Infallible Proofs*.

CHAPTER 8

THE MIRACULOUS PRONOUNCEMENT OF JOHN'S BIRTH

But the angel said, "Don't be afraid, Zechariah! God has heard your prayer. Your wife, Elizabeth, will give you a son, and you are to name him John."　　Luke 1:13

One of the strangest events of the early gospel narrative is the sudden appearance of a man, out of the desert wilderness. He was known as John the Baptist. He was the son of Zachariah (or Zacharias), a priest, and his wife Elizabeth, a daughter of the line of high priests stemming from Aaron, the brother of Moses. His parents were related

> He [Gabriel] said that because of the righteousness, obedience and unfailing prayer of this couple, God had heard their pleas and would reward them with a son!

to the parents of Jesus. Elizabeth was Mary's cousin. God chose to honor this holy family with another miracle child. Everything about John's birth and life was miraculous, and provided many signs for the people of that day and for the people of all times to come.

ELIZABETH'S BARRENNESS REMOVED

Elizabeth was barren and elderly as well, but the same angel Gabriel who visited Mary visited Zacharias as he was ministering in the Temple and spoke to him. He said that because of the righteousness, obedience and unfailing prayer of this couple, God had heard their pleas and would reward them with a son.

This promised son would not be a normal child in any sense of the word:

"You will have great joy and gladness, and many will rejoice at his birth, for he will be great in the eyes of the Lord. He must never touch wine or other alcoholic drinks. He will be filled with the Holy Spirit, even before his birth."
Luke 1:14-15

"Many will rejoice at his birth."
"He will be great in the eyes of the Lord."
"He will be filled with the Holy Spirit, even before his birth."

These are not normal things in any sense of the word, and yet the most important thing the angel Gabriel said that day was this:

"And he will turn many Israelites to the Lord their God.
He will be a man with the spirit and power of Elijah.
He will prepare the people for the coming of the Lord.
He will turn the hearts of the fathers to their children,
and he will cause those who are rebellious to accept the
wisdom of the godly." Luke 1:16-17

Zacharias was dumbfounded by this pronouncement. Could these things be true? Was he having delusions? Was he dreaming? He was an old man and not at all sure that he was even capable of siring a child. His wife, too, was *"well along in years"*:

Zechariah said to the angel, "How can I be sure this
will happen? I'm an old man now, and my wife is also
well along in years." Luke 1:18

Could Zachariah and Elizabeth still produce a son at their age? Surely he was justified to question it and to insist, *"How can I be sure this will happen?"* But God apparently was not pleased with Zechariah's answer. He was expecting more faith from such a spiritual man. Gabriel answered him in this unusual way:

> *"I am Gabriel! I stand in the very presence of God. It was he who sent me to bring you this good news! But now, since you didn't believe what I said, you will be silent and unable to speak until the child is born. For my words will certainly be fulfilled at the proper time."*   Luke 1:19-20

This phase, *"you will be silent,"* is translated by the New King James Version as *"you will be mute"* and by the original King James Version as *"thou shalt be dumb."* The meaning is clear. A prominent priest, a man who served God and the people through his speaking would now suddenly find himself unable to speak.

This muteness which Zechariah would experience, however, would be temporary. *"You will be mute until the day these things take place"* declares the New King James Version. *"You will be silent and unable to speak until the child is born,"* declares the New Living Translation. Both prophetic predications are detailed and very specific.

THE MIRACULOUS OUTCOME

Amazingly, when Zacharias left the Temple that day, he could not speak to those who waited for him. He motioned to them, trying to explain what he had seen and heard. They were unable to understand what he was trying to convey to them and came to their own conclusions about what had transpired in the Temple that day:

Meanwhile, the people were waiting for Zechariah to come out of the sanctuary, wondering why he was taking so long. When he finally did come out, he couldn't speak to them. Then they realized from his gestures and his silence that he must have seen a vision in the sanctuary.

Luke 1:5-22

Being unable to speak, how was Zechariah able to communicate to his beloved wife the shock of what he had just experienced? Did he, perhaps, write it out for her to read? Or was he somehow able to make himself understood in other ways? Amazingly, people who love each other have more than mere words to communicate their thoughts. What is clear is that Elizabeth, too, came to understand the message of the angel, and she became part of its fulfillment:

When Zechariah's week of service in the Temple was over, he returned home. Soon afterward his wife, Elizabeth, became pregnant and went into seclusion for five months. "How kind the Lord is!" she exclaimed. "He has taken away my disgrace of having no children." Luke 1:23-25

There were no complaints, only rejoicing. God had chosen this godly couple to bring a very special person into the world for a very special task. These elderly people were not dismayed by this turn of events in any way. They were ecstatic.

Where were the scribes and Pharisees when all of this was taking form? Could they have been ignorant of such things? Never! Rather, these men willfully and knowingly chose to reject God's *Infallible Proofs*.

CHAPTER 9

MORE MIRACULOUS CONFIRMATIONS FOR MARY AND FOR ELIZABETH

"Behold, thy cousin Elisabeth, she hath also conceived a son in her old age: and this is the sixth month with her, who was called barren. For with God nothing shall be impossible." Luke 1:36-37

According to the words of Gabriel to Zechariah, his barren wife Elizabeth would now miraculously conceive. As we noticed, this same angel Gabriel was the messenger who visited the mother of Jesus, the virgin Mary, and told her that she, too, would bear a child and that He would be the Savior of the world.

TWO MIRACULOUS SONS

Did Mary and Elizabeth just happen to be related? Or did faith and obedience to God run in this family? Whatever the case, the Lord chose to visit these cousins with two miraculous sons—one to the barren and one to the virgin.

Gabriel first visited Zacharias and made his pronouncement concerning the birth of John. Then, when he visited Mary, it was already in the sixth month of Elizabeth's pregnancy. Neither Zacharias nor Elizabeth had told anyone what the Lord had promised them, and after her conception, Elizabeth had hidden herself, so that absolutely no one knew that she was expecting. In his message to Mary, however, Gabriel confirmed his message to Zacharias, telling her that her cousin was also expecting a child.

MARY'S MIRACULOUS VISIT

Mary decided to visit her cousin, to confirm the message of Gabriel, so she made a hurried journey into the hill country, to a Judean village where Elizabeth was in seclusion. When she arrived at the place, something very unusual happened. When Elizabeth heard the greeting of Mary, her (Elizabeth's) unborn child leaped in her womb and she (Elizabeth) was simultaneously filled with the Holy Spirit and began to prophesy with a loud voice:

> *"God has blessed you above all women, and your child is blessed. Why am I so honored, that the mother of my Lord should visit me? When I heard your greeting, the baby*

in my womb jumped for joy. You are blessed because you believed that the Lord would do what he said."

Luke 1:42-45

This is the only recorded instance of someone leaping for joy before birth, but it happened. The unborn prophet leaped for joy at the presence of his Savior (Jesus was already growing in the womb of Mary).

Mary had spoken only a word of greeting—nothing more—and yet, without another word, the Spirit of God revealed to Elizabeth that her cousin Mary was bearing the Lord and Savior in her body.

SEEMINGLY CONTRADICTORY STATEMENTS

The first two statements Elizabeth made may have seemed contradictory. She knew that her cousin Mary was not yet married, yet despite that knowledge, she prophesied, *"God has blessed you above all women, and your child is blessed."* The New King James Ver-

When Elizabeth heard the greeting of Mary, her unborn child leaped in her womb, and she was simultaneously filled with the Holy Spirit and began to prophesy!

sion renders this phrase as *"blessed is the fruit of your womb."* But what was a blessed, unmarried woman doing with a *"fruit of the womb?"*

Was Elizabeth taking a great responsibility upon herself by saying these things? No, she surely wasn't. She was not speaking of herself. It was the Holy Spirit who had come upon her that was doing the speaking. Elizabeth would never have dared say such a thing, even if she had expected it for some reason. But the power of God suddenly came upon her, and she spoke without fear what seemed to be a preposterous prophecy. It was not preposterous at all. Everything that Elizabeth said was true, and it was a powerful confirmation to Mary that what the angel had told her was indeed from God.

No one had known the details of it all except Joseph and Mary. Now, however, the Lord showed Elizabeth. In the same way, no one had known about Elizabeth's pregnancy except she and Zacharias, but the Lord had now shown Mary. In this way, these two cousins were able to comfort each other with their miraculous confirmations, very obviously from the Lord.

Mary remained in the house of Elizabeth for about three months, then returned to her own home sometime before John was born.

So Few Were Willing to Believe

It is possible that neither Many nor Elizabeth shared their secrets with others, but if that is true, it was only because so few were willing to believe and so many wanted to do harm to God's servant John and His Beloved Son Jesus. Far too many men willfully and knowingly rejected God's *Infallible Proofs*.

CHAPTER 10

THE MIRACULOUS BIRTH AND YOUNG LIFE OF JOHN THE BAPTIST

When it was time for Elizabeth's baby to be born, she gave birth to a son. Luke 1:57

Elizabeth delivered a son, as the angel had foretold. When her neighbors and relatives heard about the miraculous birth, they all rejoiced. The Lord had shown mercy upon their beloved Elizabeth:

And when her neighbors and relatives heard that the Lord had been very merciful to her, everyone rejoiced with her. Luke 1:58

A MIRACULOUS NAME

> The Lord had spoken to both Elizabeth and Zacharias, on separate occasions, and given them the identical name for their child!

According to Jewish ceremony, a child was named on the eighth day, the day of circumcision, and so everyone gathered on that day to decide on a proper name for Elizabeth's son. They decided to call him "*Zechariah*" after his father:

When the baby was eight days old, they all came for the circumcision ceremony. They wanted to name him Zechariah, after his father.
Luke 1:59

Elizabeth protested:

"No! His name is John!"
Luke 1:60

The others argued:

"What? ... There is no one in all your family by that name."
Luke 1:61

Seeing how utterly adamant Elizabeth was being on this matter, the people decided to let Zechariah settle the argument (if he could), and so they asked him what he wanted to name the child. Zachariah motioned for a writing table and wrote on it these simple words:

"His name is John."   Luke 1:63

This amazed everyone who was present to witness it:

So they all marveled.   Luke 1:63, NKJ

The Lord had spoken to both Elizabeth and Zacharias, on separate occasions, and given them the identical name for their child. In the very same way, the Lord had instructed Mary and Joseph, also on separate occasions, to name their child *"Jesus"*:

As he considered this, an angel of the Lord appeared to him in a dream. "Joseph, son of David," the angel said, "do not be afraid to take Mary as your wife. For the child within her was conceived by the Holy Spirit. And she will have a son, and you are to name him Jesus, for he will save his people from their sins."   Matthew 1:20-21

"Don't be afraid, Mary," the angel told her, "for you have found favor with God! You will conceive and give birth to a son, and you will name him Jesus.   Luke 1:31

They were both miraculous names given in miraculous ways.

THE FULFILLMENT OF ZECHARIAH'S TIME

There was another important miraculous element in the naming ceremony. When Zechariah wrote on the table the phrase, *"His name is John,"* he completed the instructions of Gabriel in the Temple. The angel had said that Zechariah would be unable to speak *"until the day these things take place [be performed, KJV]"* (Luke 1:20, NKJ). The giving of the name *"John"* was the last *"thing"* that was to *"be performed."* When Zechariah had done this, *"Instantly [he] could speak again [for the first time in nine months], and he began praising God"* (Luke 1:64). The result of these amazing occurrences was this:

> *Awe fell upon the whole neighborhood, and the news of what had happened spread throughout the Judean hills. Everyone who heard about it reflected on these events and asked, "What will this child turn out to be?" For the hand of the Lord was surely upon him in a special way*
>
> . Luke 1:65-66

WHAT IT MEANT TO COME "IN THE SPIRIT OF ELIJAH"

When Zechariah first encountered the angel in the Temple, he probably understood little of the significance of the messenger's words. His only surprise seemed to be that he could have a child in his old age. The words of Gabriel, however, were much more significant. Theologians, knowing well the prophecies of Malachi, believed that the prophet Elijah would return to Judea just before the coming of the Messiah and would introduce the Savior to the Jewish people:

"Look! I am sending my messenger, and he will prepare the way before me. Then the Lord you are seeking will suddenly come to his Temple. The messenger of the covenant, whom you look for so eagerly, is surely coming," says the Lord of Heaven's Armies. Malachi 3:1

"Look, I am sending you the prophet Elijah before the great and dreadful day of the Lord arrives. His preaching will turn the hearts of fathers to their children, and the hearts of children to their fathers. Otherwise I will come and strike the land with a curse." Malachi 4:5-6

It is recorded that Elijah, who lived some nine centuries before Christ, did not die a physical death, but was taken up to Heaven alive by the Lord:

When the Lord was about to take Elijah up to heaven in a whirlwind, Elijah and Elisha were traveling from Gilgal. 2 Kings 2:1

As they were walking along and talking, suddenly a chariot of fire appeared, drawn by horses of fire. It drove between the two men, separating them, and Elijah was carried by a whirlwind into heaven. 2 Kings 2:11

The angel Gabriel stated that John would have *"the spirit and power of Elijah"* and would prepare the people of

Israel for the coming of the Messiah. John, then, was the fulfillment of Malachi's prophecy. Jesus confirmed this when, speaking to His disciples about who John really was, He said:

"John is the man to whom the Scriptures refer when they say,

'Look, I am sending my messenger ahead of you,
and he will prepare your way before you.'

"I tell you the truth, of all who have ever lived, none is greater than John the Baptist. Yet even the least person in the Kingdom of Heaven is greater than he is! And from the time John the Baptist began preaching until now, the Kingdom of Heaven has been forcefully advancing, and violent people are attacking it. For before John came, all the prophets and the law of Moses looked forward to this present time. And if you are willing to accept what I say, he is Elijah, the one the prophets said would come. Anyone with ears to hear should listen and understand!"

Matthew 11:10-15

ZACHARIAS' UNDERSTANDING

Whether Zacharias came to understand this more fully during the following months before his child was born we cannot be sure, but on the eighth day of the child's life, when he had obeyed Gabriel in the final point, naming his son John, the tongue of Zacharias was loosed, he was *"filled with the Holy Spirit"* (Luke 1:67), and he prophesied these amazing words:

"Praise the Lord, the God of Israel, because he has visited and redeemed his people.
He has sent us a mighty Savior from the royal line of his servant David,
just as he promised through his holy prophets long ago.
Now we will be saved from our enemies and from all who hate us.
He has been merciful to our ancestors by remembering his sacred covenant—
the covenant he swore with an oath to our ancestor Abraham.
We have been rescued from our enemies so we can serve God without fear, in holiness and righteousness for as long as we live." Luke 1:68-75

> *When he had obeyed Gabriel in the final point, naming his son John, the tongue of Zacharias was loosed, he was "filled with the Holy Spirit," and he prophesied!*

139

ADDRESSING HIS NEWBORN SON

Turning then and addressing his newborn son directly, Zechariah prophesied further:

"And you, my little son,
will be called the prophet of the Most High,
because you will prepare the way for the Lord.
You will tell his people how to find salvation
through forgiveness of their sins.
Because of God's tender mercy,
the morning light from heaven is about to break upon us,
to give light to those who sit in darkness and in the shadow
of death,
and to guide us to the path of peace."   Luke 1:76-79

Just a moment before, this man had been mute and unable to speak. Now he was prophesying the future.

Maybe it was only now, after Zechariah had been *"filled with the Holy Spirit,"* that this significant revelation came to him. His son was an anointed prophet of the Lord, miraculously conceived and born, who would introduce the long-awaited Messiah to the people of Israel. Modern-day prophets are often just as amazed as anyone else at what comes out of their mouths. This probably was true for Zechariah, as well.

JOHN'S YOUNG LIFE

It is said of John, as it was said of Jesus, that as a child he *"became strong in spirit"* (Luke 1:80). This same verse tells us most of what else we know about his young life:

And he lived in the wilderness until he began his public ministry to Israel.

It is possible that John's parents died when he was very young. At an early age, he entered the desert wilderness (very possibly to live with the ascetic Essene group at their Qumran commune near the Dead Sea). Whether this part of the story is true or not, John remained in the desert, communing with God, eating locusts and wild honey, wearing a crude garment woven from camel's hair and a leather sash around his waist, until he was about thirty:

John grew up and became strong in spirit. And he lived in the wilderness until he began his public ministry to Israel. Luke 1:80

And the same John had his raiment of camel's hair, and a leathern girdle about his loins; and his meat was locusts and wild honey. Matthew 3:4

It was at this point that John emerged to begin his ministry, preaching to the people of Israel to repent and baptizing them unto that repentance. We will note the many miraculous aspects of this ministry in the next chapter.

Jesus and John both had miraculous parents, miraculous births, miraculous names, and miraculous childhoods, all leading to miraculous lives and ministries.

141

How could anyone alive in that day have remained ignorant of these things? No, like it or not, the religious leaders of Jesus' day were hypocrites, for they willing and knowingly ignored these *Infallible Proofs*.

CHAPTER 11

MIRACULOUS SIGNS IN JOHN'S MINISTRY

In those days John the Baptist came to the Judean wilderness and began preaching. His message was, "Repent of your sins and turn to God, for the Kingdom of Heaven is near."   Matthew 3:1-2

John was very bold to denounce the hypocrisy of the Sadducees and Pharisees, as Jesus later did:

But when he saw many Pharisees and Sadducees coming to watch him baptize, he denounced them. "You brood of snakes!" he exclaimed. "Who warned you to flee God's coming wrath? Prove by the way you live that you have repented of your sins and turned to God. Don't just say

to each other, 'We're safe, for we are descendants of Abra-
ham.' That means nothing, for I tell you, God can create
children of Abraham from these very stones."

Matthew 3:7-8

This was serious business, and John quickly put everyone on notice of that fact. Despite the harshness of his
message, however, perhaps because of the many signs
accompanying his birth and young life, he was well accepted as a prophet sent from God:

People from Jerusalem and from all of Judea and all over
the Jordan Valley went out to see and hear John. And when
they confessed their sins, he baptized them in the Jordan
River.   Matthew 3:5-6

This was a large area to cover by foot, showing that
the influence of John was vast, a direct fulfillment of the
prophecies of both Gabriel and Zacharias and of the prophetic pronouncements of the Old Testament.

WHY WAS HE CALLED THE BAPTIST?

When John saw true signs of repentance in his followers, he asked them to confess their sins and submit to
water baptism. This was the practice that earned him the
name The Baptist.

Many of the followers of John believed that he was
himself the Christ. He strongly denied that, saying:

"I baptize with water those who repent of their sins and turn to God. But someone is coming soon who is greater than I am—so much greater that I'm not worthy even to be his slave and carry his sandals. He will baptize you with the Holy Spirit and with fire. He is ready to separate the chaff from the wheat with his winnowing fork. Then he will clean up the threshing area, gathering the wheat into his barn but burning the chaff with never-ending fire."

Matthew 3:11-12

"I baptize with water, but right here in the crowd is someone you do not recognize. Though his ministry follows mine, I'm not even worthy to be his slave and untie the straps of his sandal."

John 1:26-27

INTRODUCING JESUS

Because of the many signs accompanying his birth and young life, he [John] was well accepted as a prophet sent from God!

The very next day, as crowds gathered again to hear his preaching, John looked up and saw Jesus coming toward him. Gesturing to the crowd, he said:

145

"Look! The Lamb of God who takes away the sin of the world! He is the one I was talking about when I said, 'A man is coming after me who is far greater than I am, for he existed long before me.' I did not recognize him as the Messiah, but I have been baptizing with water so that he might be revealed to Israel." John 1:29-31

This was the moment for which John had been born, and because of his popularity, he was now able to introduce the nation to its Messiah, as had been foretold.

JOHN HAD NEVER SEEN JESUS BEFORE

John said something else very interesting that day. This phrase, *"I did not recognize him as the Messiah,"* is translated in the New King James as, *"I did not know Him."* In other words, this was the first time the two of them had met.

Because their mothers were cousins, many would reject immediately John's claim that he had not previously known Jesus. We must remember, however, that travel was uncommon in those days, and the homes of Jesus and John were at least fifty miles apart. Jesus lived in Galilee and John in Judea.

We must also consider the fact that John entered the wilderness at a very early age and remained there until his preaching ministry began. Jesus worked in Joseph's carpenter shop in Nazareth until about the same time.

As John saw Jesus approaching Jordan's banks, he had only the witness of the Spirit to tell him that this was *"the Lamb of God."* Their paths had never crossed since the time their pregnant mothers spent together in Judea. Even as he had leaped for joy that first day in his mother's womb, now John again supernaturally recognized his Lord and Savior, the object of his life and ministry.

JUST HOW DID JOHN RECOGNIZE JESUS?

How did John recognize Jesus? In answer to that question, he said:

"I saw the Spirit descending from heaven like a dove, and He remained upon Him."   John 1:32

It was a miraculous revelation that he could now share with many others, and he did so with great power.

Think about it! On that day alone, John was able to reveal the Christ to the inhabitants of Jerusalem, Judea and the regions around the Jordan River—an amazing fulfillment of prophecy. Tell me, where were the scribes and Pharisees when all of this was happening? They must have been very busy back in Jerusalem doing whatever they did. They were far too busy to be there on this all-important day. No wonder Jesus called them *"an evil, adulterous generation."* They willfully and knowingly rejected His *Infallible Proofs.*

CHAPTER 12

JESUS' MIRACULOUS BAPTISM

*After his baptism, as Jesus came up out of the water,
the heavens were opened and he saw the Spirit of God
descending like a dove and settling on him. And a
voice from heaven said, "This is my dearly loved Son,
who brings me great joy."* Matthew 3:16-17

What John saw that day (before baptizing Jesus)
was just the beginning of a whole series of miraculous
signs God would give concerning His Son. Perhaps
others did not see the first one John saw, but they
would soon see for themselves the proofs that Jesus
was Lord and King.

JESUS' REQUEST TO BE BAPTIZED

> John was convinced that the baptism of Jesus was necessary as an example to others, so he obeyed and baptized the Son of God!

When Jesus requested John to baptize Him also, John tried to refuse, feeling that he needed be baptized by Jesus. But Jesus insisted, stating that He must set an example for others:

But Jesus said, "It should be done, for we must carry out all that God requires." So John agreed to baptize him. Matthew 3:15

Although the New Living Translations renders Jesus' reason that convinced John, *"We must carry out all that God requires,"* the New King James Version translates it as, *"It is fitting for us to fulfill all righteousness."* Jesus had not sinned that He should require new birth, and baptism is symbolic of that new birth. Paul taught the Roman believers:

For we died and were buried with Christ by baptism. And just as Christ was raised from the dead by the glorious power of the Father, now we also may live new lives.
Romans 6:4

John was convinced that the baptism of Jesus was necessary as an example to others, so he obeyed and baptized the Son of God in the sight of the great throng of people present that day.

More Miraculous Signs

After the baptism was accomplished, and as Jesus was coming up out of the water, it appeared to all that a dove, a symbol of God's Spirit, suddenly flew down and landed on Him. At the same instant, a voice was heard from Heaven saying, *"This is my dearly loved Son, who brings me great joy"* (Matthew 3:17). John then told the people that God had earlier spoken to him and told him what to look for, and how he had seen it:

> *"I saw the Holy Spirit descending like a dove from heaven and resting upon him. I didn't know he was the one, but when God sent me to baptize with water, he told me, 'The one on whom you see the Spirit descend and rest is the one who will baptize with the Holy Spirit.' I saw this happen to Jesus, so I testify that he is the Chosen One of God."*
>
> John 1:33-34

How could John have possibly been more clear and precise? And what more could God have done to put His stamp of approval upon Jesus?

A dove appearing and alighting on Him, a voice being heard from Heaven, and that voice declaring that Jesus was God's dearly loved Son, John knowing a man he had never seen before ... all these signs were unmistakable and miraculous confirmations from Heaven, *Infallible Proofs,* that Jesus Christ was the Son of the living God. Still, some religious leaders continued to ask Him for a sign. How blind could they be?

Just the day before, some Pharisees and Sadducees had appeared in the crowd that followed John, and he had turned to address them openly and frankly (see Matthew 3:7). Among the things he told them was that very *"soon"* the Greater One was coming, and the next day it all happened. Had none of the religious leaders returned that day to see what was about to happen? Apparently not. They felt secure in their religiosity. How very sad!

THE SCENE NOW SHIFTS

Before long John was placed in prison by Herod the Tetrarch, also known as Herod Antipas. He was not the same Herod who had the Judean children massacred. That was his father. Herod Antipas' reasons for having John imprisoned were not founded on legal grounds. Rather, he was angry because John had publicly criticized him:

> *John also publicly criticized Herod Antipas, the ruler of Galilee, for marrying Herodias, his brother's wife, and for many other wrongs he had done. So Herod put John in prison, adding this sin to his many others.*   Luke 3:19-20

Jesus continued to preach for the next three years throughout Judea and Galilee, and so the scene suddenly shifted, and the major characters changed.

Why did this happen? John had been born for a divine purpose, and that divine purpose had now been fulfilled. He had experienced his hour, and his hour had now passed. As he himself noted, a *"greater"* than he had appeared, and now the popular ministry of John must not be allowed to compete with the emerging ministry of Jesus. So God removed him from the scene in this very convenient way.

Of course, this didn't seem fair. What had John done to deserve it? And this bothered him. In prison, he proved his humanity, for at one point, he sent disciples to Jesus asking if he was really the Christ or if they should look for another:

> *John the Baptist, who was in prison, heard about all the things the Messiah was doing. So he sent his disciples to ask Jesus, "Are you the Messiah we've been expecting, or should we keep looking for someone else?"*
>
> Matthew 11:2-3

All of us experience moments of weakness, and this was John's moment. Jesus, however, did not rebuke him or remind him of all that God had revealed to him and allowed him to reveal to the nation. He simply answered with something he knew John would understand:

> *Jesus told them, "Go back to John and tell him what you have heard and seen — the blind see, the lame walk, the*

lepers are cured, the deaf hear, the dead are raised to life, and the Good News is being preached to the poor. And tell him, 'God blesses those who do not turn away because of me.' "   Matthew 11:4-6

Signs and wonders was definitely something that John could understand.

JESUS' OPINION OF JOHN

As the disciple of John were leaving to bear this message to him, Jesus turned to the crowd and began to speak to them of John. Nothing that He said that day was negative. This great man may have had a weak moment, but he was still a great man:

"What kind of man did you go into the wilderness to see? Was he a weak reed, swayed by every breath of wind? Or were you expecting to see a man dressed in expensive clothes? No, people with expensive clothes live in palaces. Were you looking for a prophet? Yes, and he is more than a prophet. John is the man to whom the Scriptures refer when they say,

'Look, I am sending my messenger ahead of you, and he will prepare your way before you.'

"I tell you the truth, of all who have ever lived, none is greater than John the Baptist. Yet even the least person in the Kingdom of Heaven is greater than he is! And from

the time John the Baptist began preaching until now, the Kingdom of Heaven has been forcefully advancing, and violent people are attacking it. For before John came, all the prophets and the law of Moses looked forward to this present time. And if you are willing to accept what I say, he is Elijah, the one the prophets said would come. Anyone with ears to hear should listen and understand!

Matthew 11:7-15

Was anyone listening that day? If they were, the scribes, Pharisees and Sadducees were not among them. They were blinded to all these supernatural happenings. They willingly and knowingly rejected God's *Infallible Proofs*.

It must be noted that John was never free to preach again, and eventually he gave his life for the sake of the Gospel. What a privilege! What a great man! What great signs God showed through him! One day we will meet him in Heaven, for he has preceded us there.

CHAPTER 13

MIRACULOUS SIGNS IN JESUS' MINISTRY

Amazed, the people exclaimed, "What authority and power this man's words possess! Even evil spirits obey him, and they flee at his command!" The news about Jesus spread through every village in the entire region.

Luke 4:36-37

During the next three years Jesus offered such signs as these:

Turning water into wine	John 2:7-10
Feeding multitudes	Matthew 14:15-21, Mark 6:34-44, Mark 8:1-9, Luke 9:12-17 and John 6:5-13

Walking on the sea	Matthew 14:25, Mark 6:48 and John 6:19
Calming a storm at sea	Mark 4:39 and Luke 8:24
Opening blind eyes	Matthew 9:29-30, Matthew 30:34, Mark 8:25, Mark 10:52, Luke 7:21 and John 9:7
Unstopping deaf ears	Mark 7:35 and Mark 9:25-27
Loosing mute tongues	Matthew 9:33, Matthew 12:22, Matthew 15:30 and Luke 11:14
Healing a paralytic	Matthew 8:6-7, Matthew 9:6-7, Mark 2:10-12 and Luke 5:24-25
Cleansing lepers	Matthew 8:2-3, Mark 1:40-42, Luke 5:13 and Luke 17:12-14
Casting out a legion of demons	Mark 5:8-13 and Luke 8:27-33
And even raising the dead	Matthew 9:24-26, Mark 5:39-42, Luke 7:12-15, Luke 8:52-55 and John 11:43-44

Wow! But all of that still wasn't enough for the religious leaders of the day. They kept rigfht on seeking more signs.

THE MIRACULOUS WISDOM AND POWER JESUS POSSESSED

One of the greatest signs that God gave the people of Israel and their leaders was the otherworldly wisdom and power that Jesus possessed and constantly demonstrated:

Everyone spoke well of him and was amazed by the gracious words that came from his lips. "How can this be?" they asked. "Isn't this Joseph's son?"   Luke 4:22

There, too, the people were amazed at his teaching, for he spoke with authority.   Luke 4:32

Much of this happened before the sequence of Matthew 12, and yet the religious leaders were still seeking a sign. In Matthew 16, we see the same men *"tempting"* the Lord, desiring a sign from Heaven. Again, Jesus rebuked them, saying:

"You know the saying, 'Red sky at night means fair weather tomorrow; red sky in the morning means foul weather all day.' You know how to interpret the weather signs in the sky, but you don't know how to interpret the signs of the times!"
     Matthew 16:2-3

> *All of that still wasn't enough for the religious leaders of the day. They kept seeking more signs!*

With reason, Jesus called these insincere leaders *"an evil, adulterous generation"* and declared that no further sign would be given to them except, as He had promised, *"the sign of the prophet Jonah"* (Matthew 16:4).

THIS ATTITUDE WAS FORETOLD

The prophet Isaiah foretold the attitude these religious leaders would have:

"This fulfills the prophecy of Isaiah that says,

'When you hear what I say,
you will not understand.
when you see what I do,
you will not comprehend.
For the hearts of these people are hardened,
and their ears cannot hear,
and they have closed their eyes—
so their eyes cannot see,
and their ears cannot hear,
and their hearts cannot understand,
and they cannot turn to me
and let me heal them.' "   Matthew 13:14-15

Here He was quoting from Isaiah 6:9-10.
'These people honor me with their lips,
but their hearts are far from me.
Their worship is a farce,
for they teach man-made ideas as commands from God.'
                                  Matthew 15:8-9

Here He was quoting from Isaiah 29:13.

The Jewish leaders knew these scriptures well, and yet they refused to recognize that Jesus was the fulfillment of them. Therefore, He described them well, when He said:

"Every plant not planted by my heavenly Father will be uprooted, so ignore them. They are blind guides leading the blind, and if one blind person guides another, they will both fall into a ditch."   Matthew 15:13-14

Jesus proceeded to pronounced eight woes upon the scribes and Pharisees (see Matthew 23). The first one was this:

"What sorrow awaits you teachers of religious law and you Pharisees. Hypocrites! For you shut the door of the Kingdom of Heaven in people's faces. You won't go in yourselves, and you don't let others enter either."
Matthew 23:13

Jesus warned the Pharisees that the dead of Nineveh would rise up on the Judgment Day and condemn their generation:

"The people of Nineveh will stand up against this generation on judgment day and condemn it, for they repented of their sins at the preaching of Jonah. Matthew 12:41

In the year 862 B.C., the Lord had determined to send judgment upon the wicked city of Nineveh. First, however, He sent the prophet Jonah to warn the people of their

When Jonah arrived in Nineveh and delivered his message of judgment, the inhabitants repented and turned to God, and, in this way, the judgment was averted!

impending doom. When Jonah arrived in Nineveh and delivered his message of judgment, the inhabitants repented and turned to God, and, in this way, the judgment was averted:

When God saw what they had done and how they had put a stop to their evil ways, he changed his mind and did not carry out the destruction he had threatened. Jonah 3:10

Jesus continued:

"Now someone greater than Jonah is here—but you refuse to repent." Matthew 12:41

Jesus further warned the Pharisees that the Queen of Sheba would rise up in the Judgment and condemn their doubting generation:

"The queen of Sheba will also stand up against this generation on judgment day and condemn it, for she came from a distant land to hear the wisdom of Solomon." Matthew 12:42

This queen visited Jerusalem in the year 992 B.C. and was deeply impacted by what she saw in King Solomon. His wisdom was otherworldly, and nothing could explain it but that it was from Heaven. He was said to be the wisest man of his time, so it's no wonder that she was impressed.

Jesus continued:

"Now someone greater than Solomon is here—but you refuse to listen."   Matthew 12:42

How blind these people were! Jesus was surely justified in refusing to give them any further sign on this occasion. The many signs already given had been ignored. These religious leaders deserved no further sign. They only deserved woe and judgment.

Jesus did promise them, however, that He would give one great sign, the one He called *"the sign of the prophet Jonah."* He admonished them to watch for this sign, desiring that many would be convinced by it and would turn to Him and live.

To this point, however, they had willfully and knowingly chosen to ignore all of the *Infallible Proofs* He was so graciously presenting.

PART THREE

GOD'S OVERRIDING MERCY

CHAPTER 14

JUSTICE DELAYED

Don't be misled—you cannot mock the justice of God. You will always harvest what you plant. Those who live only to satisfy their own sinful nature will harvest decay and death from that sinful nature. But those who live to please the Spirit will harvest everlasting life from the Spirit.

Galatians 6:7-8

God is a just God, a God of true judgment. He rewards people according to their deeds. The Apostle Paul wrote:

But God shows his anger from heaven against all sinful, wicked people who suppress the truth by their wicked-ness.

Romans 1:18

Because of these sins, the anger of God is coming.

Colossians 3:6

The King James Version renders it in this way:

For which things' sake the wrath of God cometh on the children of disobedience:

> **God metes out just rewards, but He is also a God of extreme love and forbearance!**

Paul wrote to the Ephesian believers:

Don't be fooled by those who try to excuse these sins, for the anger of God will fall on all who disobey him. Ephesians 5:6

Yes, God metes out just rewards, but He is also a God of extreme love and forbearance:

The Lord isn't really being slow about his promise, as some people think. No, he is being patient for your sake. He does not want anyone to be destroyed, but wants everyone to repent. 2 Peter 3:9

Our Lord is ever willing to give us another chance, there being always the possibility that some may repent of their evil doings and turn to Him. The prophet Moses wrote:

The Lord is slow to anger and filled with unfailing love,
forgiving every kind of sin and rebellion.

Numbers 14:18

The Psalmist, King David, sang:

The Lord is compassionate and merciful,
slow to get angry and filled with unfailing love.
He will not constantly accuse us,
nor remain angry forever.
He does not punish us for all our sins;
he does not deal harshly with us, as we deserve.
For his unfailing love toward those who fear him
is as great as the height of the heavens above the earth.

Psalm 103:8-11

Despite the attitude of the contentious religious leaders of Jesus' day, and although He had only promised them one more sign (*"the sign of the prophet Jonah"*), the mercy of God prevailed for them. The Almighty not only gave them the one great sign He had repeatedly promised, but also a whole series of great signs centering around the death of Jesus. These signs were (and still are) further proof that He was and is the only begotten Son of God, God Himself veiled in human flesh, the Savior of the world.

HOW GOD SPOKE TO THESE PEOPLE

So that He would not be misunderstood, God spoke to the people of Jesus' day in terms directly relating to their religion. He could not have done that in countries where only a few knew anything about their faith. But He could do it in Israel. Indeed, that was the best way to speak to the Jewish people, for their religion was their life. Because of this, God gave them signs involving sacred beliefs, sacred places, sacred items and sacred rituals. These were signs that could not go unnoticed and would be difficult to ignore.

Religious observance in Israel revolved around the Temple. This huge building was patterned after a plan God had given to Moses on Mount Sinai for the building of the wilderness Tabernacle (see Exodus 25-27). The Temple consisted of three main areas. The largest of these was called the Outer Court. Next, came the Holy Place. And the smallest and most sacred area was known as the Most Holy Place or the Holy of Holies. It was there in that most intimate part of the Temple that the sacred Ark of the Covenant was kept.

THE ARK OF THE COVENANT

The Ark of the Covenant was a large wooden box overlaid with gold inside and out. It contained the tables of stone on which God Himself had written the ten basic commandments of the Law. At one time the Ark also contained a shepherd's rod which God miraculously caused to bring forth buds (a reminder to Israel of the rebellion of her ancestors in the wilderness), and a container with manna that God had given miraculously to feed His people in the wilderness (a reminder of God's unfailing provision for His own).

On top of the Ark rested the Mercy Seat, and upon that Mercy Seat the High Priest sprinkled the blood of animal sacrifices once a year for the sins of the people. The Mercy Seat was made of pure gold, and on each side of it stood a golden cherub (angel).

THE VEIL OF THE TEMPLE

The Most Holy Place was separated from the rest of the Temple by a thick veil made of several interwoven pieces of material. God described it in this way:

"For the inside of the Tabernacle, make a special curtain of finely woven linen. Decorate it with blue, purple, and scarlet thread and with skillfully embroidered cherubim." Exodus 26:31

Once a year, the High Priest took a blood sacrifice into the Most Holy Place and sprinkled it on the Mercy Seat. The sins of the people were thus covered over for the past year, and they could began the new year with a clean slate.

THE GUARDIANS OF THE TEMPLE

The Temple was kept holy by men dedicated to the priesthood. They were all descendants of Aaron, brother of Moses:

THE SCENE IS SET

These details provide the setting for a whole series of miraculous signs that God was about to give to His people, more of His *Infallible Proofs*.

CHAPTER 15

MIRACULOUS SIGNS DURING JESUS' ARREST AND TRIAL

Then the high priest stood up and said to Jesus, "Well, aren't you going to answer these charges? What do you have to say for yourself?" But Jesus remained silent. Then the high priest said to him, "I demand in the name of the living God—tell us if you are the Messiah, the Son of God."

Jesus replied, "You have said it. And in the future you will see the Son of Man seated in the place of power at God's right hand and coming on the clouds of heaven." Then the high priest tore his clothing to show his horror and said, "Blasphemy! Why do we need other witnesses? You have all heard his blasphemy. What is your verdict?"

"Guilty!" they shouted. "He deserves to die!"

Then they began to spit in Jesus' face and beat him with their fists. And some slapped him, jeering, "Prophesy to us, you Messiah! Who hit you that time?"

Matthew 26:62-68

From the very beginning of Jesus' ministry here on earth, the religious leaders of His day had frequently sought to discredit Him. They could not explain the amazing things He was doing and the powerful way He was speaking and, because they were unwilling to accept Him for who He said He was, they constantly sought ways to do Him harm. Eventually this led to His arrest and trial.

MIRACULOUS SIGNS DURING THE BETRAYAL

Judas, one of Jesus' chosen disciples, betrayed Him:

The traitor, Judas, had given them a prearranged signal: "You will know which one to arrest when I greet him with a kiss." So Judas came straight to Jesus. "Greetings, Rabbi!" he exclaimed and gave him the kiss.

Matthew 26:48-49

Jesus was not at all surprised by this and answered Judas in this way:

"My friend, go ahead and do what you have come for."

Matthew 26:50

It had been evident from His birth that Jesus had come to die, so He counted as *"friend"* those who were involved

174

in His capture. His time was at hand, and those who sought to do Him harm were, in reality, just facilitating His destiny. To prove this, He offered no resistance and reproved those of His disciples who did:

> *Then the others grabbed Jesus and arrested him. But one of the men with Jesus pulled out his sword and struck the high priest's slave, slashing off his ear.*
>
> *"Put away your sword," Jesus told him. "Those who use the sword will die by the sword. Don't you realize that I could ask my Father for thousands of angels to protect us, and he would send them instantly? But if I did, how would the Scriptures be fulfilled that describe what must happen now?"* Matthew 26:50-54

Jesus was ready for *"what must happen now,"* even if His disciples were not. Dying for the sins of all men everywhere was the very reason He had come to Earth, and this would be His final triumph.

It had been evident from His birth that Jesus had come to die, so He counted as "friend" those who were involved in His capture!

As He was being arrested, He made yet another effort to reach out to and reason with those who were accusing Him:

Then Jesus said to the crowd, "Am I some dangerous revolutionary, that you come with swords and clubs to arrest me? Why didn't you arrest me in the Temple? I was there teaching every day. But this is all happening to fulfill the words of the prophets as recorded in the Scriptures."
Matthew 26:55-56

What these men were doing didn't make sense, but Jesus was able to make perfect sense of it. It was all part of the Father's plan of redemption for all mankind.

Attached to this last verse was a very sad footnote:

At that point, all the disciples deserted him and fled.
Matthew 26:56

You would have thought that these men who had been with Jesus now for more than three years would know enough to stand. You would think that they had seen enough of His power to cause them to know that He was always in control and that whatever happened now was for their best and for the benefit of His Kingdom. But, alas, they were all too human. They *"deserted him and fled."*

THE GRAND SCHEME

The capture of Jesus was all part of a grand scheme, and the very religious leaders who had developed it were, at that very moment, gathered, waiting for Him to be brought before them:

> *Then the people who had arrested Jesus led him to the home of Caiaphas, the high priest, where the teachers of religious law and the elders had gathered.*
>
> Matthew 26:57

Jesus would be tried, not before a Roman court of law, but before the very religious leaders who hated Him. He would stand before the Jewish High Council, made up of the current high priest, Caiaphas, other leading priests, principle teachers of the Law and elders of the people.

THE FALSE WITNESSES

The next part of the plot was about to unfold. It involved calling in several false witnesses and having them speak against Jesus. This backfired when the witnesses who had been convinced to lie against Him contradicted each other:

> *The leading priests and the entire high council were trying to find witnesses who would lie about Jesus, so they could put him to death. But even though they found many who agreed to give false witness, they could not use anyone's testimony.*
>
> Matthew 26:59-60

Eventually they found two men who said they had heard Jesus threaten to tear down the Temple:

Finally, two men came forward who declared, "This man said, 'I am able to destroy the Temple of God and rebuild it in three days.' " Matthew 26:60-61

> **The question had been direct, and the answer was even more direct. Yes, Jesus was the Christ!**

That seemed like very damning evidence, so Caiaphas asked Jesus what He had to answer to such a serious charge, but Jesus declined to answer:

Then the high priest stood up and said to Jesus, "Well, aren't you going to answer these charges? What do you have to say for yourself?" But Jesus remained silent.
Matthew 26:62-63

Tired of beating around the bush, Caiaphas next asked the question that all Israel wanted to know, the reason for the trial in the first place:

"I demand in the name of the living God — tell us if you are the Messiah, the Son of God."
Matthew 26:63

Jesus answered this question in the very simplest way possible:

"You have said it."   Matthew 26:64

Then Jesus went on to make another of His amazing claims:

"And in the future you will see the Son of Man seated in the place of power at God's right hand and coming on the clouds of heaven."   Matthew 26:64

The question had been direct, and the answer was even more direct. Yes, Jesus was the Christ. He was the promised Messiah. He was the Son of God. When Caiaphas heard this answer, his response was very strange:

Then the high priest tore his clothing to show his horror.   Matthew 26:65

To a casual Bible reader, this might not seem significant. After all, rending or tearing your clothes was a common practice in Bible days. It denoted sorrow and mourning. Many great figures in Bible history had been known to do this same thing, for example:

Reuben	Genesis 37:29
Jacob	Genesis 37:34
Joseph's brothers	Genesis 44:13
Joshua and Caleb	Numbers 14:6
Joshua and the elders	Joshua 7:6

Jephthah	Judges 11:35
Mordecai	Esther 4:1
Job	Job 1:20

Many kings of Israel tore their clothes in times of great sorrow. For example:

David	2 Samuel 13:31
Ahab	1 Kings 21:27
Josiah	2 Chronicles 34:19

Many prophets did the same thing. For example:

| Elisha | 2 Kings 2:12 |
| Ezra | Ezra 9:5 |

Way back in the early 1960's I was challenged by a respected Asian Indian pastor to discover the true significance of Caiaphas' act. He felt that it had been against the Law of Moses for the high priest to tear his garments. I didn't know if it had or not, but I became interested enough to find out. As I studied in the books of Law, I found the following passages which show that the priest's garments were considered sacred or "*holy*":

> "*Then take some of the blood from the altar and some of the anointing oil, and sprinkle it on Aaron and his sons and on their garments. In this way, they and their garments will be set apart as holy.*"   Exodus 29:21

Next Moses took some of the anointing oil and some of the blood that was on the altar, and he sprinkled them on Aaron and his garments and on his sons and their garments. In this way, he made Aaron and his sons and their garments holy.   Leviticus 8:30

"He must put on his linen tunic and the linen undergarments worn next to his body. He must tie the linen sash around his waist and put the linen turban on his head. These are sacred garments, so he must bathe himself in water before he puts them on."   Leviticus 16:4

In the book of Ezekiel, I found the following reference:

"When the priests leave the sanctuary, they must not go directly to the outer courtyard. They must first take off the clothes they wore while ministering, because these clothes are holy. They must put on other clothes before entering the parts of the building complex open to the public."
                                        Ezekiel 42:14

I also found that the priestly garments were made so that they would not accidentally tear:

"Reinforce the opening with a woven collar so it will not tear."   Exodus 28:32

The opening was reinforced with a woven collar so it would not tear.   Exodus 39:23

181

Then I found what I had been looking for. Yes, the priests were actually forbidden to tear these holy garments:

> Then Moses said to Aaron and his sons Eleazar and Ithamar, "Do not show grief by leaving your hair uncombed or by tearing your clothes. If you do, you will die, and the Lord's anger will strike the whole community of Israel. However, the rest of the Israelites, your relatives, may mourn because of the Lord's fiery destruction of Nadab and Abihu.   Leviticus 10:6

As I continued to study, I found it to be true that, although kings and prophets had often torn their garments in sorrow, never in the history of the Jewish race had a high priest desecrated the sacred garments of the priesthood in this manner. These garments were passed down from one generation of high priests to the next:

> "In future generations, the purification ceremony will be performed by the priest who has been anointed and ordained to serve as high priest in place of his ancestor Aaron. He will put on the holy linen garments."
>   Leviticus 16:32

> There you will remove Aaron's priestly garments and put them on Eleazar, his son. Aaron will die there and join his ancestors."
> So Moses did as the Lord commanded. The three of them went up Mount Hor together as the whole community

watched. At the summit, Moses removed the priestly garments from Aaron and put them on Eleazar, Aaron's son. Then Aaron died there on top of the mountain, and Moses and Eleazar went back down.
                                Numbers 20:26-28

Because the priestly garments were to be passed down from one generation to another, they were never to be torn or altered or desecrated in any way. They became the symbol of an *"everlasting priesthood"*:

"Anoint them as you did their father, so they may also serve me as priests. With their anointing, Aaron's descendants are set apart for the priesthood forever, from generation to generation."   Exodus 40:15

"In this covenant, I give him [Phineas, grandson of Aaron] and his descendants a permanent right to the priesthood, for in his zeal for me, his God, he purified the people of Israel, making them right with me."   Numbers 25:13

> *Because the priestly garments were to be passed down from one generation to another, they were never to be torn or altered or desecrated in any way!*

Because of this, I am sure that Caiaphas must have wondered what possessed him to do such a rash thing, and I am equally sure that the Council knew the Law and understood the grave significance of this particular sign from God.

WHAT DID IT ALL MEAN?

God moved upon Caiaphas to tear his priestly garments in the presence of representatives from all the Jewish communities. By this act He was saying, "You no longer need an earthly high priest to be your intercessor before God. This Man is the Christ, the Messiah, the King. He is God's Son, your De-liverer. Jesus has now become your heavenly High Priest (see Hebrews 2:17, 3:1, 4:14, 6:20 and 8:1). By this prophetic act, Caiaphas was saying, "Jesus has become your Intercessor, and therefore the earthly priesthood is dissolved from this moment on."

In reality, Caiaphas may not have believed this in his heart, but as far as God was concerned, the line of earthly high priests came to an end with Caiaphas.

THE VERDICT OF MEN

But what was the verdict of the men involved. As far as they were concerned, Jesus was a blasphemer, a man worthy of death. Caiaphas was the first to declare it and then, when he called for a ruling from the other council members, they unanimously agreed. Let's see it all in context again:

Then the high priest tore his clothing to show his horror and said, "Blasphemy! Why do we need other witnesses? You have all heard his blasphemy. What is your verdict?" "Guilty!" they shouted. "He deserves to die!"

Matthew 26:65-66

It all happened so fast. It seems that these men didn't even consider the amazing thing that has just happened before their eyes. *"Guilty!" they shouted. "He deserves to die."* And, with that, the trial was over, and the sentencing began. These men who had witnessed so many wonderful things from the hands and lips of the Savior now suddenly began beating on Him with their fists and spitting on Him in their rage:

Then they began to spit in Jesus' face and beat him with their fists. And some slapped him, jeering, "Prophesy to us, you Messiah! Who hit you that time?"

Matthew 26:67-68

Please tell me how men could be so blind. Some might imagine that these men had never had a real opportunity to see Jesus as He truly was, but that's simply not the case. They'd had every opportunity, and yet they willingly and knowingly chose to reject God's *Infallible Proofs*.

CHAPTER 16

MIRACULOUS SIGNS DURING PILATE'S INTERROGATION OF JESUS

Very early in the morning the leading priests and the elders met again to lay plans for putting Jesus to death. Then they bound him, led him away, and took him to Pilate, the Roman governor.   Matthew 27:1-2

If these Jewish leaders could have executed Jesus, they would have, but, being under Roman rule at the time, they were deprived of the right of pronouncing the actual death sentence. But they knew how to get it done. They need only play on the weaknesses of the Roman Governor, Pontius Pilate, and that's what they now did.

As Jesus stood accused before the governor, Pilate began to question him. Strangely enough, the first question he asked Jesus was the same question that Caiaphas had asked:

> *Pilate encouraged Jesus to defend Himself, but He refused!*

"Are you the king of the Jews?" the governor asked him.
> Matthew 27:11

Jesus' answer was again short, to the point, and affirmative:

Jesus replied, "You have said it."
> Matthew 27:11

The chief priests and elders then began to make many accusations against Jesus, but He chose not to answer them. Pilate encouraged Jesus to defend Himself, but He refused. The governor marveled at this. He saw something unusual in Jesus and wanted no part of His execution. He stated emphatically to the crowd:

"I find nothing wrong with this man!"   Luke 23:4

And that should have been the end of it, but these men were not about to give up so easily. They argued with Pilate, becoming *"insistent"*:

Then they became insistent. "But he is causing riots by his teaching wherever he goes—all over Judea, from Galilee to Jerusalem!" Luke 23:5

In that moment, Pilate found the loophole he needed. If Jesus was from Galilee and a Galilean, then He belonged to the jurisdiction of Herod Antipas. Let Herod decide His fate. Conveniently, Herod was there in Jerusalem at that very moment, so the prisoner was sent to him now:

And as soon as he knew that He belonged to Herod's jurisdiction, he sent Him to Herod, who was also in Jerusalem at that time. Luke 23:7, NKJ

Strangely or not, Herod was happy to see Jesus. In fact, he was *"delighted"*:

Herod was delighted at the opportunity to see Jesus, because he had heard about him and had been hoping for a long time to see him perform a miracle. Luke 23:8

Even Herod Antipas had heard of Jesus. Everyone had. And even an evil king knew that Jesus performed miracles. Herod just wanted to see one of them for himself.

There was another reason for Herod's joy at seeing Jesus. He had long suspected that Jesus might be John the Baptist risen from the dead:

When Herod Antipas, the ruler of Galilee, heard about Jesus, he said to his advisers, "This must be John the

189

*Baptist raised from the dead! That is why he can do such
miracles."*   Matthew 14:1-2

Don't forget that it was this same Herod who had had
John beheaded.

Herod now put a series of questions to Jesus, but Jesus
"refused to answer":

*He asked Jesus question after question, but Jesus refused
to answer.*   Luke 23:9

Although it seemed inconceivable (and still does to
many today), Jesus steadfastly refused to defend Himself.
Why? Because He knew that He must die for the sins of all
mankind, and so, again, what these men were doing was
facilitating His most important work.

The religious leaders pressured Herod *"vehemently"*
(KJV), accusing Jesus:

*Meanwhile, the leading priests and the teachers of reli-
gious law stood there shouting their accusations.*
                                               Luke 23:10

Herod had his soldiers provide a kingly robe for Jesus
and allowed everyone to mock Him, but he was not ready
to sentence Jesus to death. He had lost enough sleep over the
beheading of John. This was Pilate's headache, he concluded,
so he sent Jesus back to Pilate—much to Pilate's dismay.

SENT BACK TO PILATE

Put on the spot again, Pilate thought of another possible way out of his dilemma and presented the idea to the Jewish leaders:

> *Then Pilate called together the leading priests and other religious leaders, along with the people, and he announced his verdict. "You brought this man to me, accusing him of leading a revolt. I have examined him thoroughly on this point in your presence and find him innocent. Herod came to the same conclusion and sent him back to us. Nothing this man has done calls for the death penalty. So I will have him flogged, and then I will release him."*
>
> Luke 23:13-17

Flogging Jesus should be punishment enough to satisfy them, Pilate reasoned. After all, the Man had done nothing wrong. But it soon became apparent to Pilate that no one was listening to him and that his plea was going unheard.

Then another brilliant plan occurred to him, and he was sure that this would convince them to allow Jesus to live. It was his custom to pardon and release a prisoner each year at the Feast of Passover. Since the feast was approaching, this gave him another good opportunity to release Jesus. He made a proposition to the people. He had a notorious prisoner named Barabbas, a murderer, an insurrectionist, and a general troublemaker, and he proposed to them an exchange. He did this in a way he was sure would convince them:

191

*"Which one do you want me to release to you — Barabbas,
or Jesus who is called the Messiah?"*   Matthew 27:17

Pilate earnestly hoped that this strategy would pay off.
He was troubled about this matter for several reasons. For
one thing, he knew that the charges against Jesus were
false and that Jesus was innocent:

*(He knew very well that the religious leaders had arrested
Jesus out of envy.)*   Matthew 27:18

PILATE'S GREATEST CAUSE FOR CONCERN

Pilate's greatest cause for concern, however, was this:

*Just then, as Pilate was sitting on the judgment seat, his
wife sent him this message: "Leave that innocent man
alone. I suffered through a terrible nightmare about him
last night."*   Matthew 27:19

This was all too strange! Jesus must go free! But to the
utter dismay of the already frustrated Pilate, the crowd
would not hear to it. To Pilate's shock and dismay, they
called for the release of Barabbas instead:

*The leading priests and the elders persuaded the crowd to
ask for Barabbas to be released and for Jesus to be put to
death.*   Matthew 27:20

Then a mighty roar rose from the crowd, and with one voice they shouted, "Kill him, and release Barabbas to us!"   Luke 23:18

We can only imagine how Pilate felt in that moment. These people were pressuring him to do something he clearly did not want to do.

PILATE'S PLIGHT IS COMPOUNDED

His plight was compounded further when, in desperation, he asked them the all-important question and they answered with one voice:

Pilate responded, "Then what should I do with Jesus who is called the Messiah?"
They shouted back, "Crucify him!"
Matthew 27:22

> *Pilate was horrified by all of this and he "argued with them"!*

Pilate was horrified by all of this and he *"argued with them"*:

Pilate argued with them, because he wanted to release Jesus. But they kept shouting, "Crucify him! Crucify him!"   Luke 23:20-21

Pilate's defense of Jesus did not end quickly, and it was made with great emotion:

"Why?" Pilate demanded. "What crime has he commit-
ted?"   Matthew 27:23

But the crowd could not be quieted, and they *"cried even louder,"* (KJV) and their cry did not change: *"Crucify Him! Crucify Him!"*

Luke recorded the fact that three times Pilate pleaded with the angry mob in this way, but still it was to no avail. Their minds were made up. They did not want to hear that Jesus was innocent. All that would satisfy them was for Him to die.

EVENTUALLY PILATE GAVE IN TO THEIR PLEAS

Eventually they cried out so loud that Pilate could no longer be heard, and he gave in to them. He must have hated himself for his weakness, but he surrendered to the absurd wishes of his subjects and assented to the sentence of death, death for the Son of God, the King of the Jews.

Pilate did let it be known that he was not in agreement with the demands of these people. When he could not prevail against the angry mob, he took water and publicly washed his hands, stating in the hearing of all:

"I am innocent of this man's blood. The responsibility is yours!"   Matthew 27:24

"I am innocent of the blood of this just Person. You see to it."   NKJ

JESUS WAS LED AWAY

And that was it! There was no more discussion. Now Roman soldiers took charge of Jesus. They stripped Him, put on Him a scarlet robe, placed a crown of thorns upon His head, and bowed before Him mockingly, saying, *"Hail, King of the Jews"* (Matthew 27:29). They spit on Him and struck Him on the head, took off His robe, beat Him thirty-nine times with a Roman lash, and led Him away to be crucified. For a great part of the way, He was forced to carry the heavy cross upon which He would soon die.

Roman soldiers crucified Jesus between two thieves on a small hill outside Jerusalem. It was reserved for such executions. The spot was known as Golgotha, the place of the skull, or Calavera, the place we have come to call Calvary. Please tell me how men could be so blind as to willingly and knowingly rejected God's *Infallible Proofs*. But more were soon to come.

CHAPTER 17

MYSTERIOUS DARKNESS AT NOONDAY

At noon, darkness fell across the whole land until three o'clock.   Matthew 27:45

There were several outstanding signs that accompanied the death of Jesus on the cross. The first of them was the darkness experienced at noonday.

This was not just any day. It was Friday, the first day of Passover, and it suddenly and mysteriously became dark at noon and remained dark until three o'clock that afternoon. Then it became light again until sundown.

Was there coincidentally an eclipse of the sun on the very day the Son of God was crucified? No! That could not explain it. The Passover Feast was always held during a full moon, and it is impossible to have an eclipse during a full moon. Furthermore, an eclipse of the sun never lasts for more than ten or eleven minutes, while this darkness lasted for three full hours.

Some have speculated that a storm darkened the area, but no such storm was recorded.

A period of darkness does sometimes precede an earthquake, and an earthquake did follow the strange darkness at Calvary. That was not the case this time, however, for this darkness was not limited to one area. It extended *"across the whole land"* (Matthew 27:45). This phrase, *"across the whole* land*"* may seem like a vague expression, but it is clarified in Luke's narrative of the same event. Luke used the term *"over all the earth"* (Luke 23:44, NKJ). That leaves no question. This was not a natural phenomenon. It was a supernatural darkness that covered the entire planet.

What could have caused such darkness? It was not an eclipse; it was not a storm; it was not a natural phenomenon preceding an earthquake, and it was not night on Calvary's side of the globe. Instead, it was the brightest part of the day, the time when the sun is directly overhead and bearing down the fiercest. Yet it was dark. Why? How? In answer to this questions, Luke wrote, *"And the sun was darkened"* (Luke 23:45, NKJ). Let me ask you, who has power to darken the sun but the very God who made it? It seems clear that God simply turned off the light of the sun that fateful day!

If there was such a darkness over the whole Earth, would it not be mentioned in other historical writings?

Is this just a Christian myth? It's a good question and it deserves an answer.

The answer is that this is not just a myth. The phenomena is mentioned in many Christian histories, but also in non-Christian histories, as well. Celsus, a famous opponent of Christianity in the third century, admitted the historical fact of darkness at Calvary. Tertullian, an affirmed Christian of the second century, wrote a challenging letter to his unbelieving heathen adversaries, his *Apologeticum*, a defense of Christianity written to pagan skeptics. In it, he boldly stated, *"At the moment of Christ's death, the light departed from the sun, and the land was darkened at noonday, which wonder is related in your own annals and is preserved in your archives to this day."*

The Pharisees had asked for signs. Now, at the Feast of Passover, representatives of the Jewish people from throughout the world were gathered. On the first day of the feast, suddenly it grew dark at noonday and remained dark until three o'clock that afternoon. God turned out the light on them.

Imagine what confusion must have followed. Ancient eclipses of the sun were accompanied with chaos. Some

> *The phenomena [of darkness at noonday] is mentioned in many Christian histories, but also in non-Christian histories, as well!*

people thought the world was coming to an end and killed themselves. Some dropped dead from heart attacks. Some had nervous breakdowns. Everyone was at least "shook up" by the unusual occurrence.

WHY GOD DID IT

Why did God turn out the lights that day in Jerusalem? It was not just as a sign. Isaiah leaves us a clue:

> *"When he sees all that is accomplished by his anguish,*
> *he will be satisfied.*
> *And because of his experience,*
> *my righteous servant will make it possible*
> *for many to be counted righteous,*
> *for he will bear all their sins.*
> *I will give him the honors of a victorious soldier,*
> *because he exposed himself to death.*
> *He was counted among the rebels.*
> *He bore the sins of many and interceded for rebels."*
>
> Isaiah 53:11-12

For three hours God veiled from human view the agony of Jesus. Why? Because during that time He took upon Himself the sins of all men and women of all generations, and with their sins, the accompanying curses and consequences. It was too much for men to behold, so God turned out the lights to hide the "unlovely," sin-cursed, agonizing face of His Son, the Lamb of God, as He was being slain for the sins of the world.

Could it be possible that none of the people in Jerusalem associated the strange and foreboding darkness with the man they had condemned to die that day at Golgotha? Were they so blind they didn't know that God had interrupted their feasting to confirm to them that His Son was dying for them nearby on a Roman cross? Surely not. As we shall see, what was happening was apparent to all, as it had been from the first day.

These men willingly and knowingly chose to ignore God's *Infallible Proofs.* What more could He do? Oh, He had a lot more planned for them.

CHAPTER 18

THE UNEXPLAINED RENDING
OF THE TEMPLE VEIL

*At that moment the curtain in the sanctuary of the Temple
was torn in two, from top to bottom.* Matthew 27:51

Jesus Christ bore the sins of the entire human race in
His own body on the cross. His life was given as the Lamb
of God, a sacrifice for our sins, so that we might be saved.

All major religions have incorporated a blood sacrifice into their teaching and ritual, for instinct seems
to tell people everywhere that a life must be sacri-
ficed to save a life. As the Scriptures so aptly declare:

*For without the shedding of blood, there is no forgive-
ness.* Hebrews 9:22

Thank God that He Himself offered the greatest sacrifice possible in the form of His own Son. Jesus' blood had to be shed for the remission of our sins—yours and mine.

HIS BLOOD FLOWED FROM SEVEN WOUNDS

The blood of Jesus flowed from seven wounds, and the number seven, when used in the Bible, denotes perfection. If something was done seven times, it was done perfectly. Jesus' blood flowed from the brow wounded by the thorn crown. It flowed from the back ripped apart by the merciless lash. It flowed from nail wounds in each hand and each foot. And (after He was already dead), it flowed from His spear-pierced side. In this way, Christ's blood was shed, and the needed sacrifice was given. The Lamb of God was slain for our sins, and salvation was complete.

But Jesus didn't die from loss of blood. Instead, He *"released [yielded up, NKJ] his spir-*

The shaking caused by the quake could not have torn a loose-hanging curtain while leaving the building that housed that curtain unharmed!

it" (Matthew 27:50). Jesus gave His life; it was not taken from Him by the will of men. And, at the very instant that Jesus gave His life, suddenly the veil of the Temple in Jerusalem was ripped in two from the top to the bottom. That was very significant indeed.

This veil was not a shabby piece of old material. It was a well constructed piece of handiwork, so designed that many scholars doubt the possibility of teams of horses pulling it apart:

> *For the inside of the Tabernacle, make a special curtain of finely woven linen. Decorate it with blue, purple, and scarlet thread and with skillfully embroidered cherubim.* Exodus 26:31

The torn veil was not a consequence of the earthquake (which we will presently discuss). The shaking caused by the quake could not have torn a loose-hanging curtain while leaving the building that housed that curtain unharmed.

The veil also did not rot into pieces; instead it was torn cleanly. And, furthermore, the tearing began at the top—too high for any human to reach.

Think about it: that veil was some sixty feet high. So who could have torn it? The answer is that God Himself took hold of the veil of the Temple and ripped it in two. And, because of this, a way was opened into the Most Holy Place.

THE SIGNIFICANCE OF THE TIMING

The timing of all this was significant. Jesus died and the veil was ripped open at three o'clock in the afternoon—exactly the time of the evening sacrifices in the Temple. The priests, in the performance of their duties, were standing in the Holy Place just in front of the veil when God suddenly ripped it in two. What the immediate reaction of those priests was we can only imagine. The effect this experience eventually had on them we know by reading the book of Acts:

> *So God's message continued to spread. The number of believers greatly increased in Jerusalem, and many of the Jewish priests were converted, too.* Acts 6:7

The priests, it would seem, would be the most difficult people to convince of a new truth because they were so steeped in their traditional religious teachings, and many of them had been among Jesus' fiercest critics. But something so dynamic happened to these particular priests that they were convinced that God was speaking to them about Christ, and they did not let much time slip by before they became *"obedient to the faith"* (KJV).

What was it about the experience these priests had that day which convinced them that what was happening was from God and that it concerned Jesus Christ? And, if the priests recognized this, why did others not recognize it?

WHAT DID IT MEAN?

The significance of the day's events lay in the significance of the Temple's construction and in the purpose for the Temple's divisions. The physical make-up denoted a spiritual counterpart, and the most important part of the construction was the veil itself.

The temple veil was a barrier. It kept men and women out, out of the presence of God, out of His glory. And why was that? It was because sin separated men and women from a holy God. Sin made man unworthy to approach God.

The congregation could enter only the Outer Court. Their sinfulness prevented them from advancing any closer to the Most Holy Place. The Priests, after completing various cleansing ceremonies, entered the Holy Place every day to make sacrifices. Even then, only the High Priest (who had to exercise extreme caution to keep himself from pollution) could enter the Most Holy Place, and he only once a year. That place was protected and limited, for there dwelt the Shekinah, a cloud of God's glory and symbol of His presence. God's ultimate greatness, the fullness of who He really was, was hidden by the veil.

The veil kept common men and women from ever experiencing God's presence. No common man had ever dared to violate the law forbidding them to enter the Holy of Holies. They knew that God would strike them dead on the spot if they tried it. And yet, suddenly, the barrier was removed. The veil was opened. Someone had torn it *"down the middle"* (Luke 23:45).

The priests suddenly were looking right into the very center of God's presence, and they were not struck dead! What could this mean?

THE SIGNIFICANCE OF THE TORN VEIL

First, the torn veil meant that sin had been dealt with. Joseph had been foretold by the angel that Jesus would come into the world to *"save his people from their sins"* (Matthew 1:21). Well, He had successfully wrestled with sin and had gained the victory. The awful darkness of Calvary's agony was past, and light now came to the world. Jesus had overcome all sin.

With sin removed, the need for the veil was removed. With the barrier to fellowship removed, men and women could now enter freely into the presence of God. Common people could approach a Holy God without fear. Through Christ they were now worthy to do that.

So the veil was the most important part of the Temple. It was on the veil that the temple dispensation or period was built. With the veil out of the way, the Temple became utterly meaningless, the temple dispensation was dissolved, and no one could doubt that God had done it Himself.

The Gospel message of Jesus and His disciples would now open the door freely to *"anyone [whosoever will, KJV]"* (Revelation 22:17) to come to God through the blood atonement of Christ, for no more barriers remained. What a wonderful message the veil spoke to the priests that day!

How much the priests realized at that moment we don't know, but over the next few days and weeks they must have come to realize that the veil had actually been a symbol or type of Christ:

And so, dear brothers and sisters, we can boldly enter heaven's Most Holy Place because of the blood of Jesus. By his death, Jesus opened a new and life-giving way through the curtain into the Most Holy Place.

Hebrews 10:19-20

The New King James Version of the Bible says it this way:

Therefore, brethren, having boldness to enter the Holiest by the blood of Jesus, by a new and living way which He consecrated for us, through the veil, that is, His flesh.

THE VEIL AS A SYMBOL OF CHRIST

The priests suddenly were looking right into the very center of God's presence, and they were not struck dead!

The veil's colors signified Christ's nature—the blue of His heavenly character, the red of His earthly character, and the purple between being the blending of both into true man and true God at once.

The King James Version of the Bible describes the veil of the Temple as *"a cunning work"* (Exodus 26:31). In the same way, Jesus the man and Christ (God veiled in human flesh) had been joined in a cunning demonstration of God's handiwork. By joining the two, He made Jesus Christ, the Word made flesh.

In the same way that the rending of the temple veil made a way for man to approach the Most Holy Place, the crucifixion of Jesus (the rending of His flesh) made a way for man to approach God, not just symbolically or in one place, but in reality and everywhere. Jesus died on the cross only because God had ordained it to be so. Many previous attempts had been made upon His life, but no one could kill Him before His time had come.

Now, the time had come, and God made His sacrifice. Jesus was smitten of the Father. In the same way that the veil was torn from above, so our veil, the flesh of Jesus, was torn by the hand of a loving God. And so a way was made, through Christ, into the presence and glory of the Father for everyone who would come, for all ages of time.

WHY DID OTHERS NOT IMMEDIATELY RECOGNIZE IT?

Why many others did not immediately recognize this we cannot really say for sure. One thing is certain. The message of the veil was not just for the priests in the Temple in Jerusalem. Everyone who was in Jerusalem visited the Temple during the Feast of Passover, and when they did, they saw the veil torn and the open Holy of Holies.

First, it had grown mysteriously dark for three hours. Then they had felt a great earthquake. Now they saw the veil of the Temple torn in two. By these signs, God was saying to the Jewish people (and to us today), "There is no more need for animal sacrifices. The Lamb of God has been slain. Never again will it be necessary to sprinkle the blood of animals upon the Mercy Seat. The blood of Jesus Christ has atoned once and for all and is now being sprinkled eternally upon the Mercy Seat of Heaven."

OTHER HISTORICAL VERIFICATION

Although the only other historical verification of the veil's rending I found is from Josephus, it is enough proof that no priest, no scholar, no historian has ever contradicted the Gospel account of this event. It happened!

Could it be possible, again, that those who witnessed this sign somehow failed to relate it to the man they had condemned to die just a few hours before? If so, how blind could they be? They willingly and knowingly chose to ignore these *Infallible Proofs*!

CHAPTER 19

A HIGHLY UNUSUAL EARTHQUAKE

The earth quaked, and the rocks were split.

Matthew 27:51, NKJ

When Jesus cried with a great voice (a cry of victory and conquest that we will discuss more in detail in the next chapter), suddenly the ground around Jerusalem began to quake. Matthew recorded it this way:

At that moment the curtain in the sanctuary of the Temple was torn in two, from top to bottom. The earth shook, rocks split apart, and tombs opened.   Matthew 27:51-52

"At that moment," all of this happened. Was it just a coincidence? Of course not. That moment changed history for all of us.

213

EVIDENCE REMAINS

How widespread this earthquake was we can't say for sure, and neither can we know how long it lasted. What we do know is that it was violent enough to tear some rocks in pieces and to open graves, and an earthquake that violent would have been felt by all the Jerusalem dwellers and the thousands of feast-time visitors to the Holy City. God physically shook them all in an attempt to restore their senses and show them what a mistake they had made in rejecting His Son.

In Jerusalem still today, you can see cracks in the face of Golgotha that experts call "very strange" and "proof that a great earthquake took place" there. God left one of His signs there for the ages to see.

NOTHING NATURAL ABOUT IT

But this was not just another earthquake. There was nothing natural about it. It was every bit a supernatural occurrence. We know this for several reasons. First, it was a great earthquake—great enough to tear rocks in two like paper, great enough to cause gaping holes in the rocky hillside, exposing Judean graves—and yet not another thing was disturbed. The Temple did not collapse; Jerusalem dwellings were not harmed, and the cross was not shaken out of its place. This was not natural.

The purpose of the earthquake was not to send the judgment of God upon an unbelieving people. Surely that would have been justified at the hour of Christ's death.

But that was not the case. A merciful God sent this supernatural phenomenon.

Three hours of darkness at noonday, the veil of the Temple torn in two and now an earthquake to boot. How unusual that all this should transpire at exactly the moment Jesus died, at the moment He gave a final shout!

As the priests stood in their place that day, just at the time of the evening sacrifice, suddenly they felt everything around them quake. Just as suddenly the veil of the Temple parted. And yet nothing else was harmed. No wonder many of them got the message!

EARTHQUAKES USHERED IN NEW DISPENSATIONS

In 1491 B.C., God spoke to the prophet Moses on Mount Sinai near the Red Sea and gave him a written law that ushered in a new dispensation in His relationship with His people. It is noteworthy that a great earthquake also took place there:

How unusual that all this should transpire at exactly the moment Jesus died, at the moment He gave a final shout!

All of Mount Sinai was covered with
smoke because the Lord had descended on it in the form

215

of fire. The smoke billowed into the sky like smoke from a brick kiln, and the whole mountain shook violently.

Exodus 19:18

God's people always remembered that particular earthquake as a sign accompanying their covenant with Him. In the tenth century before Christ, King David made mention of it in one of his songs:

The earth trembled, and the heavens poured down rain before you, the God of Sinai,
before God, the God of Israel.   Psalm 68:8

Earthquakes were thought of, by Jewish believers, to be connected with the presence and, even more so, the speaking of their God. For instance:

Tremble, O earth, at the presence of the Lord,
at the presence of the God of Jacob.   Psalm 114:7

I looked at the mountains and hills,
and they trembled and shook.   Jeremiah 4:24

It was only natural then for the Lord to send another earthquake—this time on Mount Calvary—to signify the ushering in of His New Covenant, a new relationship between God and man, a new dispensation of time.

The death of Jesus brought to an end the "age of law" and began the "age of grace" or the "dispensation of the Church." It brought about a new relationship between man and God. Through Christ, we can be born into the family of God. He becomes our Father, and we become His children. An earthquake and the rending of the Temple veil gave testimony to this fact.

THE CENTURION BELIEVED

There was a Roman centurion standing near the cross that day with some of his friends. They were all idolatrous men, pagan worshipers of false gods. They knew nothing of the prophets Moses or Elijah. They had never seen any of the miracles of Christ or heard any of His matchless teachings, and yet when they saw the darkness at noonday, heard the shout of Jesus from the cross, and felt the violence of the earthquake, their response was notable:

> *The Roman officer and the other soldiers at the crucifixion were terrified by the earthquake and all that had happened. They said, "This man truly was the Son of God!"*
>
> Matthew 27:54

Others who were standing by and saw it all, left *"beating their breasts"*:

> *And all the throngs that had gathered to see this spectacle, when they saw what had taken place, returned to their homes, beating their breasts.* Luke 23:48, AMP

May God help the proud Pharisees. A Roman soldier will speak against them at the Great Judgment Day. God be merciful to the scribes. A pagan knew more than they did on the day Jesus died for the sins of all mankind. How could they have been so blind as to willingly and knowingly ignore all of these *Infallible Proofs*?

CHAPTER 20

THE HIGHLY UNUSUAL CRY OF VICTORY

And Jesus cried out again with a loud voice, and yielded up His spirit. Matthew 27:50

I am totally convinced that the cry from the cross was not a normal cry from a dying man and should be listed as one of the signs from Heaven that sealed the claims of Jesus.

IT WAS UNANIMOUS

In telling about this final cry from the cross, three of the four gospel writers, Matthew, Mark and Luke, used an identical expression. That is unusual. The three men were different. They had different levels of education, different backgrounds, and different vocabularies. Although their general texts agree, often their wording is quite varied, and they tell identical stories in very different ways. In this case, however, the same wording was given to them by the Holy Spirit as they wrote. They all said Jesus *"cried out with a loud voice."*

> *Matthew and Mark noted a direct connection between the abnormally loud shout, the unusual earthquake, and the rending of the Temple veil!*

And Jesus cried out again with a loud voice, and yielded up His spirit. Matthew 27:50, NKJ

And Jesus cried out with a loud voice, and breathed His last. Mark 15:37, NKJ

And when Jesus had cried out with a loud voice, He said, "Father, 'into Your hands I commit My spirit.'" Having said this, He breathed His last. Luke 23:46, NKJ

So these three writers agree that Jesus *"cried out with a loud voice,"* but how loud is *"loud"*? I believe, from the context of these passages, that the *"loud"* spoken of here refers not to a human loudness, but to a loudness that could only be obtained, for instance, by using some sort of an amplifier. The final shout of Jesus from the cross was so loud that it merited mention by all three writers, and it brought from each of them the same expression.

THE RESULTS OF THE SHOUT

Matthew and Mark noted a direct connection between the abnormally loud shout, the unusual earthquake, and the rending of the Temple veil. They seem to be saying that the dynamic shout was the very force that shook the earth and tore the veil.

All three writers gave a direct connection between the shout and the reaction of the Centurion, his companions, and others standing near the cross. The consensus is that the shout affected everyone more than the earthquake or the darkness.

WHAT A SHOUT!

What a shout that must have been! What a glorious shout! What a shout of victory! The shout of the Conqueror. The shout of the Overcomer. And why would Jesus have shouted so?

He shouted in victory because sin was forever paid for, Satan was forever defeated, and Christ was the Victor! It was in that moment that from His lips came a shout so great that it must have been heard above the din of Jerusalem activity:

"What was that?" I imagine someone asking.

"It sounded like someone shouting."

"No man could shout that loud."

"But I heard it."

"And so did I."

And so did everyone. I'm sure of it. Maybe, with the accompanying earthquake, the shout lost some of the people's attention, but at the very least, they must have remembered it and spoken of it long afterward.

Crucified, Jesus shouted victory in His dying moment. Death was His victory. Death was His calling. Death was His crowning. So, drawing His last breath, He gave a final shout of victory that astonished everyone who heard it and everyone who heard about it.

Victory! Sweet Victory!

How could men willfully and knowingly ignore such *Infallible Proofs?*

CHAPTER 21

THE AMAZING "SIGN OF JONAH"

As the crowd pressed in on Jesus, he said, "This evil generation keeps asking me to show them a miraculous sign. But the only sign I will give them is the sign of Jonah. What happened to him was a sign to the people of Nineveh that God had sent him. What happens to the Son of Man will be a sign to these people that he was sent by God.

Luke 11:29-30

Some followers of Jesus who were noted citizens themselves went to Pilate and asked him if he would release the body of Jesus to their care. When he was certain that Jesus was dead, Pilate consented.

These disciples then wrapped Jesus' body carefully with grave clothes. They omitted much of normal embalming spices, however, because the Sabbath would soon begin:

And now when the even was come, because it was the
preparation, that is, the day before the sabbath, Joseph
of Arimathaea, an honourable counsellor, which also
waited for the kingdom of God, came, and went in
boldly unto Pilate, and craved the body of Jesus.

Mark 15:42-43

This must have been what was called a high sabbath rather than the normal Jewish Sabbath, which always began Friday at sundown. We can assume this because it was against the Law to bury the dead on the normal Jewish Sabbath.

WHERE AND HOW JESUS WAS BURIED

Prominent among the disciples who took charge of Jesus' body that day was Joseph of Arimathea, a wealthy man who owned a garden area adjacent to Golgotha's hill. There he had a partly finished tomb carved into the face of solid rock. It was a final resting place that he had been preparing for himself and his family.

It was a room, actually two rooms (an outer room and an inner room), carved into solid rock. It was clearly intended to ultimately accommodate an entire family, but only one of the spots was finished. Now Joseph's workmen quickly enlarged that one finished spot to accommodate Jesus' body, for He was taller than Joseph. When this was finished, Jesus' body was placed inside this borrowed tomb, and after rolling a great stone over the door or entrance to the rooms, the disciples departed.

THEY REMEMBERED

The following day, many Chief Priests and Pharisees again went to Pilate. They remembered the words of Jesus, Whom they called *"that deceiver,"* when He said *"After three days, I will rise again"* (Matthew 27:63). They remembered. How could they forget?

Now they wanted Pilate to put a seal on the tomb and have it guarded night and day so that no one could steal the body of Jesus and claim that He had risen. This leads me to believe that they fully understood what Jesus meant by *"the sign of Jonah."*

WHO WAS THIS JONAH?

For anyone who might not know, Jonah was a prophet of the eighth century before Christ. While running away from an assignment the Lord had given him, he was thrown over the side of a ship and swallowed by a large fish. He remained alive in the belly of the fish for three days and three nights. His ordeal is documented in the Bible book that bears his name.

> *Joseph's workmen quickly enlarged that one finished spot to accommodate Jesus' body, for He was taller than Joseph!*

225

After three days, in answer to the repentant prayer of the prophet, the fish vomited out Jonah onto the shore. Jesus said that as Jonah was in the belly of the great fish for three days, so He would be in the belly of the earth for three days. And as Jonah then came forth alive from the belly of the fish, so He would come forth alive from the grave. He had admonished the people to watch for this sign, and it is apparent that they understood what it was they were to watch for, even if they did not yet believe that it would happen. Instead, they feared that Jesus' disciples would try to "fake" a resurrection. They vowed that they would not permit this to happen. That's why they needed the tomb to be sealed and guarded.

SEALED AND GUARDED

In answer to these concerns, the authorities now sealed the tomb where Jesus lay and set a watch to guard it night and day.

So they sealed the tomb and posted guards to protect it.
Matthew 27:66

For three days the tomb remained undisturbed. Nothing seemed to be happening, and perhaps the Jewish authorities relaxed a little. But they could not relax too much, for Jesus had given three days as the period in which He would remain in the bowls of the earth. After that, He said, He would come forth—just like Jonah had.

And, sure enough, early in the morning of the fourth

day, something strange began to happen at the tomb. The Jerusalem countryside once again shook violently. Then, even as the ground continued to quake, the soldiers who were guarding the tomb witnessed a strange sight:

Suddenly there was a great earthquake! For an angel of the Lord came down from heaven, rolled aside the stone, and sat on it. His face shone like lightning, and his clothing was as white as snow. The guards shook with fear when they saw him, and they fell into a dead faint.

Matthew 28:2-4

These Roman soldiers were the best. They were chosen for their size and valor, and then trained to be the most valiant fighters in the world. But what these particular men saw that day caused them to faint dead away. How long they lay there in a dead faint we don't know, but they must have been gone by the time the women came along, for their is no mention of the two groups interacting.

THE COMING OF THE WOMEN

Several women came to the tomb early that morning bearing spices to anoint the body of Jesus. They wondered who would roll away the great stone for them, so that they could enter. To their great surprise, the door to the tomb was already open, and they could enter it freely.

When the women entered, they were dismayed and surprised to find that Jesus was no longer there. Instead, they saw an angel sitting at the head of the grave where the Lord had been lain, and they were understandably frightened.

The angel spoke to them:

"Don't be alarmed. You are looking for Jesus of Nazareth, who was crucified. He isn't here! He is risen from the dead! Look, this is where they laid his body." Mark 16:6

In spite of these comforting words, the women fled from the tomb in fear and ran to tell Jesus' disciples what they had seen and heard.

WHAT DID IT ALL MEAN?

What did it all mean to the people of that day? And what does it mean to us today? It meant simply that Jesus had fulfilled His promise. He said that He would rise again from the dead and that this would be the greatest of the signs He would offer as infallible proof that He was the Son of God, the Savior of the world. And He did just what He said, with every detail. The sign of Jonah, then, was the most powerful

In spite of these comforting words, the women fled from the tomb in fear and ran to tell Jesus' disciples what they had seen and heard!

of the many miraculous signs given to the people of that day. And it still speaks to us today.

Of the world's great religious leaders, only Jesus rose from the dead. All others died and remained dead and buried. Jesus Christ, then, is the risen and living Savior of all mankind. The sign of Jonah was given and, to draw attention to it (so that no one could later claim that they had not seen it), the sign was accompanied by an earthquake. How much more emphatic could this sign have been?

THE BRIBING OF THE ROMAN SOLDIERS

When the Roman soldiers revived from their faint, they must have gone excitedly telling others what they had seen, for the news spread quickly throughout Jerusalem that Jesus had risen from the dead.

When this news reached the religious leaders, they had a decision to make. Would they finally believe in Jesus, accepting this sign as infallible proof of who He really was? Or would they stubbornly continue to try to discredit Him and His teachings?

Their answer was not long in coming. The Jewish leaders, much to their shame, conspired to bribe the soldiers to lie, changing their story and spreading word among the people that certain disciples of Jesus had overpowered them and stolen away the body of their Master:

As the women were on their way, some of the guards went into the city and told the leading priests what had happened. A meeting with the elders was called, and they decided to give the soldiers a large bribe. They told the soldiers, "You must say, 'Jesus' disciples came during the night while we were sleeping, and they stole his body.' If the governor hears about it, we'll stand up for you so you won't get in trouble." So the guards accepted the bribe and said what they were told to say. Their story spread widely among the Jews, and they still tell it today.

Matthew 28:11-15

In this way, the religious leaders of Jesus' day rejected *"the sign of Jonah,"* the sign of all signs that Jesus was indeed Lord and Savior. And, with this reprehensible act, they also rejected their hope of eternal salvation.

What could have motivated them to reject such *Infallible Proofs?* How could they have been so blind?

CHAPTER 22

THE SUPERNATURAL ASPECTS OF JESUS' BURIAL CLOTHES

Then Simon Peter arrived and went inside. He also noticed the linen wrappings lying there, while the cloth that had covered Jesus' head was folded up and lying apart from the other wrappings. Then the disciple who had reached the tomb first also went in, and he saw and believed.

John 20:6-8

When the disciples of Jesus heard the news of His resurrection, they ran with joy to the tomb to see if all the things they had been told were true. What they found there was another great sign to them and to us and infallible proof that Jesus' body was not stolen, but that He had indeed risen from the dead.

231

WHAT PETER SAW THAT DAY

> *In some ways what was done to Jesus' body was similar to the processes used in ancient Egypt to preserve the bodies of the Pharaohs!*

Entering the tomb, the disciple Peter immediately noticed two things that were highly unusual. Lying on the flat stone surface, which had been the final resting place of Jesus, he saw, unmoved and undisturbed, the grave clothes (*"the linen wrappings"*) from Jesus' body, and he also saw *"the cloth that had covered Jesus' head."* Why were these two things significant? And why did this cause John to believe?

As mentioned earlier in the book, the Jewish dead were wrapped in linen cloth. These grave clothes came in narrow strips and were kept on long rolls. The cloth was wrapped around the body, each wrapping overlapping the last one, and there were many layers of wrapping. Between each of the layers spices were usually placed. The result was a hard shell or cocoon, much like the modern casts that are placed on broken limbs to hold them in place until the bone heals. Such a cocoon kept the body from the air, preserving it for a short period of time.

MUCH LIKE AN EGYPTIAN MUMMY

In some ways what was done to Jesus' body was similar to the processes used in ancient Egypt to preserve the bodies of the Pharaohs. There it was done even more meticulously, and the result was a mummy that would last for centuries if kept from air and light. Such mummies are still being discovered in ancient tombs and being extensive studied with modern techniques. Only very recently new studies have shown how and why King Tut died so young.

In other ways, the analogy does not apply to Jesus. We know, for instance, that His body did not have all the usual spices applied to it, but it did have the seemingly endless wrappings of linen.

You may recall that He had been similarly wrapped at birth, signifying that He was born to die. Now, thirty-three years later, He was again been wrapped in grave clothes, for He *had* died as He must. But He had also risen from the dead, as He said He would. Death and the grave could not hold Him. Then, somehow, He also escaped from the binding cocoon that had enclosed his body.

What Peter saw in the tomb that day was the undisturbed cocoon that had held his Lord. Because of the lack of spices it may have been flexible and somewhat collapsed, but it was unmoved and no one had unwrapped it. There was no opening in it large enough for a human body to go out through. It was solid except for the opening at the neck.

THE HEAD WRAPPING

There was another difference between the mummies of Egypt and the Jewish tradition of burial. The head of the mummies was also encased in the hardened shell of wrappings and spices. The Jews, however, used a larger piece of cloth for the head and folded it around the head, rather than wrap it.

The head of Jesus, then, had been wrapped with a separate linen *"napkin,"* and now Peter and the others found that napkin lying in its place at the head of the grave clothes. The napkin or head cloth had not been moved, and it was still folded, as it had been the night before. Yet the body it had enfolded was gone.

This was all conclusive proof to Peter that Jesus was alive, and seeing this sign caused John to believe. It was just that powerful!

Despite these (and all the other) signs, however, many remained unmoved. How utterly blind could they be? How could they willfully and knowingly reject such *Infallible Proofs*?

CHAPTER 23

THE AMAZING RISEN SAINTS

The bodies of many godly men and women who had died were raised from the dead. They left the cemetery after Jesus' resurrection, went into the holy city of Jerusalem, and appeared to many people. Matthew 27:52-53

If it were not enough that Jesus Himself rose from the dead, surely this next sign should have convinced even the greatest of skeptics.

THE CONNECTION WITH THE CROSS

To understand this sign completely, we must look back at the cross. Something that happened there paved the way for this highly usual occurrence. When Jesus gave the great shout, resulting in the earthquake, the rending of the temple veil, and the splitting of the rocks around Jerusalem, another result was that many surrounding rocky tombs were split open. Let's look at that passage one more time:

And Jesus cried out again with a loud voice, and yielded up His spirit. Then, behold, the veil of the temple was torn in two from top to bottom; and the earth quaked, and the rocks were split, and the graves were opened; and many bodies of the saints who had fallen asleep were raised, and coming out of the graves after His resurrection, they went into the holy city and appeared to many.

Matthew 27:51-52, NKJ

So these graves were split open when Jesus died, and then, when He arose, others arose with Him.

WHAT A STRANGE OCCURRENCE!

The fact that graves had suddenly cracked open must have been noised abroad as a weird and frightening occurrence accompanying the death of Jesus, but the real purpose of the opened graves and their effect on the people was not felt for several days.

Then, on that glorious morning, when the resurrection power of God descended into the sealed tomb of Joseph of Arimathea and raised Jesus from the dead (triumphant over death, Hell and the grave), some of that power splashed over onto other opened graves, and other dead people were resurrected.

236

THE AMAZING RISEN SAINTS

GOD RAISED UP DEAD PEOPLE AND THEY WERE RECOGNIZED

God raised up dead people and sent them into the Holy City, where many saw them and were witnesses to this phenomenon. How many other peoples rose from the dead we are not told, and neither are we told who exactly they were. All that we know is that they were *"saints,"* and that simply means believers. The New Living Translation calls them *"godly men and women who had died."* We can also surmise that these were Jewish saints who had not been dead very long, for when they appeared in Jerusalem, they were recognized. What could all that signify?

Peter and John were able to recognize Moses on the Mount of Transfiguration, although he had been dead for centuries, but Peter and John had their spiritual eyes open, whereas so many of the Jewish people of Jesus' day had even their natural eyes blinded. They would not have recognized ancient prophets, and yet they knew and recognized these saints who had risen

> *God raised up dead people and sent them into the Holy City, where many saw them and were witnesses to this phenomenon!*

237

from the dead. God knew just what to do to reach them, and yet they failed to accept His signs for the infallible proofs they were.

AN ACCUMULATED RESPONSIBILITY

Were these religious leaders just innocent people who were misunderstanding the situation? That doesn't seem possible. They had sought a sign from God concerning the Messiah—something they could see, something they could hear, or something they could feel. In response the Lord gave them the many signs of Christ's miraculous birth, miraculous growth, and miraculous ministry. When they were yet dissatisfied, He gave them these signs: the rending of the High Priest's garments contrary to sacred law, three hours of darkness at midday to accompanying the sufferings of Jesus, the rending in two from top to bottom of the veil of the Temple, two earthquakes in a period of three days, cracked rocks and subsequent opened graves, and the resurrection of Jesus itself with its accompanying proofs. When they had rejected all of this and still spoke of Jesus as a *"deceiver"* and *"blasphemer,"* God, in His mercy, raised up dead men and sent them into Jerusalem as witnesses of the power of His Son. I ask you, what further proof could anyone possibly ask for? And how could men and women willfully and knowingly reject such *Infallible Proofs*?

CHAPTER 24

THE UNFORGETTABLE SIGN OF PENTECOST

On the day of Pentecost all the believers were meeting together in one place. Suddenly, there was a sound from heaven like the roaring of a mighty windstorm, and it filled the house where they were sitting. Then, what looked like flames or tongues of fire appeared and settled on each of them. And everyone present was filled with the Holy Spirit and began speaking in other languages, as the Holy Spirit gave them this ability. Acts 2:1-4

After His resurrection, Jesus remained on the earth for forty days in His glorified body, appearing to many disciples and proving to them that He was alive:

> *They would then be anointed to preach with the same wisdom and power with which He had preached and to pray for the sick and cast out demon spirits!*

During the forty days after his crucifixion, he appeared to the apostles from time to time, and he proved to them in many ways that he was actually alive. And he talked to them about the Kingdom of God.

Acts 1:3

WHAT WAS NEXT FOR THE DISCIPLES?

After this, Jesus instructed His followers to go into Jerusalem to an upper room, where they were to wait until He sent them the power of the Holy Spirit. Once this power came upon them, they would then be anointed to preach with the same wisdom and power with which He had preached and to pray for the sick and cast out demon spirits, just as He had done while He was here on Earth. In other words, His anointing would come upon them, and they would begin to do His work in earnest.

The occasion upon which God chose to give this miraculous blessing (the power of the Holy Spirit) was very significant for those humble believers, and it was also another opportunity for non-believers to accept God's Son. It was the Day of Pentecost, and on that day, God's people celebrated in Jerusalem the second most important of their yearly feasts (after Passover). As a consequence, nearly as many gathered for this feast as for the Feast of Passover.

WHAT WAS PENTECOST?

Pentecost is a Greek term meaning fifty, and the Feast of Pentecost was celebrated fifty days after Passover. It was a celebration of the grain harvest and was one of only three occasions on which all males were required to appear before the Lord at the Temple in Jerusalem. Therefore people traveled there from many areas of the known world. Another successful harvest proved to all that God was able to sustain His people.

The ceremony that evolved through centuries came to be known as *Shavuot*. It is a time of much rejoicing and of sacrifices and prayers to God. Since it is traditionally believed that Moses brought the Ten Commandments down from Mt. Sinai fifty days after the original Passover in Egypt, over time this feast became a commemoration of the covenant God struck with man in that place.

For Christians, Pentecost signifies the miracle of the birth of the church, and it is a dramatic affirmation that God's plan of redemption applies to all the people of the world—not just the Jews. The giving of the Holy Spirit to mere mortals that day brought the dawn of a new age in which believers were encouraged to become witnesses to the people around them until the Gospel message has been preached to the ends of the earth.

WHO WAS THERE THAT DAY?

So who was present in Jerusalem on this particular Pentecost when God chose to display His power in a new and unusual way? Besides the people of Jerusalem and the surrounding Jewish areas, the Jews of the dispersion who were present that day were named as being: Parthians, Medes, Elamites, Romans, Cretes, Arabians, and the people of Mesopotamia, Cappadocia, Pontus, Phrygia, Pamphylia, Egypt, and Libya (see Acts 2:9-11). In other words, there was a good representation from the entire Jewish world. When they had all gathered in the Holy City, God chose that time and place to give one last great sign.

Now, as the humble believers of Christ prayed together in the upper room, something unusual began to happen. Not only did these believers begin speaking in strange languages; they were also noisy and acting in a strange and exuberant manner. The noise they were making was heard throughout much of the city (despite the commotion of the feasts), and throngs of people gathered to see what was happening. What they saw and heard amazed them.

WHAT THEY SAW AND HEARD

About a hundred and twenty men and women were speaking new languages, and all one hundred and twenty of them were Galileans and knew well only the dialect of Galilee. Among them were fishermen, tax collectors, other common laborers and women. None of them was well educated, and yet, as they spoke, those who gathered to listen understood what was being said. How could this happen? Ignorant and unlearned men and women, all the disciples of Jesus, were speaking fluently the difficult languages of the representative nationalities.

Let's look at that passage one more time, this time with more context:

> *They were completely amazed. "How can this be?" they exclaimed. "These people are all from Galilee, and yet we hear them speaking in our own native languages! Here we are—Parthians, Medes, Elamites, people from Mesopotamia, Judea, Cappadocia, Pontus, the province of Asia, Phrygia, Pamphylia, Egypt, and the areas of Libya around Cyrene, visitors from Rome (both Jews and converts to Judaism), Cretans, and Arabs. And we all hear these people speaking in our own languages about the wonderful things God has done!"* Acts 2:9-11

This great miracle was another sign given specifically for these Jewish people, but aside from the fact that unlearned Galileans were speaking in many foreign languages, what the disciples were saying in those languages added authenticity to the miracle of their speaking. And what were they speaking?

243

*"And we all hear these people speaking in our own lan-
guages about the wonderful things God has done!"*

What could be more powerful?

THE FIRST REACTION OF THE MULTITUDE

The first reaction of the multitude was that the disciples were drunk, but others of them quickly realized that
drunken persons could never speak languages they had
never learned.

Simon Peter, one of Jesus' disciples and a former fisherman from the Galilee, now stood up, lifted his voice above
the crowd, and spoke to the people. He showed them that
what they were seeing and hearing was not the result of
wine, but was a direct fulfillment of the words of their
prophet Joel (who lived eight hundred years before Christ):

*"These people are not drunk, as some of you are assuming.
Nine o'clock in the morning is much too early for that. No,
what you see was predicted long ago by the prophet Joel.*

*'In the last days,' God says,
'I will pour out my Spirit upon all people.
Your sons and daughters will prophesy.
Your young men will see visions,
and your old men will dream dreams.
In those days I will pour out my Spirit
even on my servants—men and women alike—
and they will prophesy.' "*   Acts 2:15-18

"PEOPLE ... , LISTEN!"

Peter began this message with these all-important words:

People of Israel, listen!   Acts 2:22

What Peter was about to say was of such consequence that it demanded the full attention of the people. God had done this thing for them, and they needed to know exactly why.

For the most part, Peter's message to the Jewish people that day was very positive. He did denounce them for attempting to kill Jesus, but he emphasized that their scheme had failed because God had raised Jesus up according to the ancient prophecies of the patriarch, King David:

> *Others of them quickly realized that drunken persons could never speak languages they had never learned!*

"I see that the Lord is always with me.
I will not be shaken, for he is right beside me.
No wonder my heart is glad, and my tongue shouts his praises!
My body rests in hope.

245

For you will not leave my soul among the dead
or allow your Holy One to rot in the grave.
You have shown me the way of life,
and you will fill me with the joy of your presence."

Acts 2:25-28

But the main point of Peter's message that day was this:

"God publicly endorsed Jesus the Nazarene by doing powerful miracles, wonders, and signs through him, as you well know."   Acts 2:22

Peter ended his message with these words:

"So let everyone in Israel know for certain that God has made this Jesus, whom you crucified, to be both Lord and Messiah!"   Acts 2:36

For some reason, those words had an impact on the hearers that nothing else previously had. When these people who had gathered that day heard such words coming from the mouth of an ignorant and unlearned fisherman, they were shocked. Luke, to show the reaction of the crowd, said, when writing the Acts of the Apostles, *"They were pricked in their heart"* (Acts 2:37, KJV). The New Living Version says it this way:

Peter's words pierced their hearts.   Acts 2:37

Finally! It was about time! Through the anointed preaching of Peter, the veil of darkness was suddenly lifted from many and their eyes were opened. They suddenly realized what hypocrites they had been and how much they needed the Savior they had slain. Was it too late? They began to cry out:

And they said to him [Peter] and to the other apostles, "Brothers, what should we do?"   Acts 2:37

Peter's answer show us God's love for every man, even for those who hate Him and His message. Peter now told them how they, too, could receive not only Christ as their Savior, but also the same gift of the Holy Spirit's power that the disciples had received:

"This promise is to you, and to your children, and even to the Gentiles—all who have been called by the Lord our God."   Acts 2:39

When the crowd had gladly received the gracious words of Peter, three thousand of them publicly accepted Christ and were baptized that day. Thank God! From that point on, thousands more responded day by day, as the message continued to be preached.

But not everyone believed. Josephus recounts in his histories that the veil of the Temple was mended, and life, for far too many Jews, went on, more or less as usual in the Holy City, Jerusalem. How could men and women be so blind? How could they willfully and knowingly choose to ignore such powerful and undeniable, *Infallible Proofs?*

PART FOUR

WHAT ABOUT YOU?

CHAPTER 25

WHAT WILL YOU DECIDE ABOUT JESUS?

Don't be misled—you cannot mock the justice of God. You will always harvest what you plant. Those who live only to satisfy their own sinful nature will harvest decay and death from that sinful nature. But those who live to please the Spirit will harvest everlasting life from the Spirit.

Galatians 6:7-8

I know that I'm repeating the opening verses of Chapter 14, but I have done it on purpose. We have seen clearly in the pages of this book that many of the religious leaders of Jesus' day chose to ignore the obvious signs from Heaven given to declare who He was and what He had come to do here. But we need to bring this message into the twenty-first century. The scribes and Pharisees of old are all gone and have long ago had to face the Judge of all the Earth. But you and I are still living. It's our turn to decide.

So what about you, dear reader? What will you decide about Jesus? Is He worthy of your honor, worthy of your praise, worthy of your sacrifice? Far too many now call themselves Christians but continue to live their lives as they wish, not as He wills.

It's very easy to criticize and think badly of the people of Jesus' day because they failed to recognize His *Infallible Proofs* and to surrender to His Lordship and do His will on a daily basis, but are we any different today? Surely no one would dare to argue that God has ceased to give us signs and wonders to reveal His power. Nothing could be further from the truth. He continues to display His glory all around us in so many different ways. Will we also remain blinded to His truth?

What is your decision today, my friend. Will you willfully and knowingly ignore God's *Infallible Proofs?*

To them also He showed Himself alive after His passion (His suffering in the garden and on the cross) by [a series of] many convincing demonstrations [unquestionable evidences and INFALLIBLE PROOFS], appearing to them during forty days and talking [to them] about the things of the kingdom of God.

Acts 1:3, AMP

To whom also he shewed himself alive after his passion by many INFALLIBLE PROOFS, being seen of them forty days, and speaking of the things pertaining to the kingdom of God:

KJV

During the forty days after his crucifixion, he appeared to the apostles from time to time, and he proved to them in many ways that he was actually alive. And he talked to them about the Kingdom of God.

NLT

MINISTRY PAGE

Readers may contact Harold McDougal in any of the following ways:

Harold McDougal
18896 Greenwell Springs Road
Greenwell Springs, LA 70739

hmcdougal@bellsouth.net

www.thepublishedword.com

www.ingramcontent.com/pod-product-compliance
Lightning Source LLC
LaVergne TN
LVHW011323080426
835513LV00006B/167